Praise for
Mr. Catherine

Mr. Catherine, Stacey Margaret Jones' exquisitely written thriller about a missing wife, is multi-dimensional, tortured and utterly believable. The main character's quiet voice hooks the reader from the page one. Deftly crafted, *Mr. Catherine* will keep you up late into the night pondering the missteps we all take and the chances for redemption we all seek.

— JENNIE FIELDS, Author of *The Age of Desire*

An intimate, psychologically acute exploration of more than one kind of mystery. Stacey Margaret Jones compels the reader with the hope of discovering the truth behind a beloved woman's disappearance, then deftly reveals the truths we hadn't thought to consider, the disappearances we've failed to notice. At once a page-turner and a perceptive, sensitive meditation on marriage and identity, guilt and forgiveness, *Mr. Catherine* is a terrific debut by Jones.

— TRENTON LEE STEWART, New York Times best-selling author of *The Mysterious Benedict Society* and *The Secret Keepers*

A blood-thrumming thriller and a wise study of middle-class contemporary marriage, Mr. Catherine is a page-turning debut that is both entertaining and heartbreaking. Stacey Margaret Jones takes the age-old tale of a fallen woman and drives a compelling and disturbing plot in a finely observed world of conservative southern America.

Jones paces her protagonist's eight-day journey of terror with precision. Her storytelling skills will leave you surprised with compassion for her flawed characters and a map of Little Rock, Arkansas, etched for all time on the back of your hand. A memorable story of ego and identity, forgiveness and revenge.

— REBEKAH CLARKSON, author of *Barking Dogs*

Mr. Catherine is a masterpiece of a first novel. It has everything a reader could possibly ask for: suspense, surprise, high drama, and high stakes. Stacey Margaret Jones has written not just a gripping mystery tale about the suspicious disappearance of a prominent businesswoman, her husband's desperate search to find her, and the criminal elements he must eventually contend with, but she has at the same time created a profoundly insightful depiction of the human complications of marriage: its disappointments and betrayals, but also its marvelous new directions, the many manners in which love can change and deepen us, in ways we could never expect.

This book is a pure pleasure and a real achievement, one that issues notice: This is a writer to watch.
  —JOHN VANDERSLICE, author of *The Last Days of Oscar Wilde*

Stacey Margaret Jones should be proud of this debut. *Mr. Catherine* is a murder mystery with Southern ambience. The sense of place infused the story with such energy I felt like I was living in Arkansas as I was reading. And the narrator—I never knew how much to trust him (and his version of Catherine) until I finished the last page.
  — SHADY COSGROVE, author of *What the Ground Can't Hold*

A page-turner of psychological intrigue that delivers more questions than answers about what unravels and then hopes to heal a wounded marriage.

In the expert hands of author Stacey Margaret Jones, it soon becomes clear that there is not just one mystery to solve, not just one missing person to save. There may be more than one murder to prevent or put to justice. Even for an expert psychotherapist such as Mr. Catherine, though, grief is complicated. Trust is elusive. And his taking action to find his beloved wife may put her at the greatest risk!
  — NANCY FREUND, author of *Rapeseed*

Mr. Catherine

Mr. Catherine

Stacey Margaret Jones

Creators Publishing
Hermosa Beach, CA

MR. CATHERINE
Copyright © 2019 Creators Publishing

Cover art by Peter Kaminski

Ted Kooser's poem, "After Years," is from his book "Delights and Shadows," published by Copper Canyon Press, www.coppercanyonpress.org. It is here used by permission of the author.

CREATORS PUBLISHING
737 3rd St
Hermosa Beach, CA 90254
310-337-7003

Library of Congress Control Number: 2019933646
ISBN (print): 9781949673067
ISBN (ebook): 9781949673074

First Edition
Printed in the United States of America
1 3 5 7 9 10 8 6 4 2

For my husband, Jay,

who always makes everything better

Contents

Prologue

There are things I didn't want to know, things I wanted to know but didn't ask, and there is the thing I didn't know was coming that I wish I could have known most of all. Perhaps I could have been more of the man I needed to be, instead of the man I am.

Day One

1

IT WAS TWO DAYS before the one-year anniversary of Catherine's confession when she didn't come home from her early morning run.

She'd gotten up as usual at 5 a.m. to run four miles, and though she had said the night before she'd use the treadmill, I found her in the kitchen assembling her outdoor gear for a run along the river trail.

I didn't usually get up that early, but the dogs were restless, and she was noisy making her to-go coffee.

"There's coffee for you, too, and the dogs were out, but Wesley may need to go again," she said. "I got up and saw the fog. It's so thick, like a big gray cushion," she said, answering my quizzing look as she led me to the window. "I just love how it's blanketing the hill. It's like the clouds don't want to get up this morning. So I'm going down to the river."

She finished her coffee ministrations.

"I love the fog!" She sang out to me over her shoulder as she passed from the kitchen into the garage. I shut the door for her, as her hands were full of a water bottle, Chomps, her iPhone, earplugs, a fleece.

That was the last time I saw her, the last time I heard her voice.

For a run of that distance, she was usually walking in the door an hour later, and I was in the shower at 6:30. At 7 a.m., I called her phone, wondering what had happened. She was going to be late for work if she didn't come home soon. When it went right to voicemail, I hung up without leaving a message, but I texted her, writing, "Almost finished? Work is waiting."

My phone stayed silent. The house, too, was still and tense. Even the dogs froze as they watched me pace from the kitchen to the picture window and back, my phone always in-hand. In January, Little Rock is gray and brown, the grass frozen but uncovered by snow, everything dead but without the pretty white shroud of winter. By now, cars were starting to go down our street toward the turn to Riverdale or the turns to Cantrell. They rolled through the dingy suburbanscape. None of them were Catherine's.

Ten minutes later, I called again. Again, straight to voicemail. The message I had sent her wasn't listed as received in the text chain. I got a cold, hard feeling in my stomach. I was both worried about her and afraid she was with the man she had cheated on me with, though that had been more than a year ago. It had always been so hard to reach her during those months. Why wasn't she home? Why wasn't she answering my calls? My text? Even if you were fucking someone, you could stop to write a text, I thought. I shook my head to get rid of the vision, the idea, the fear.

I walked out on the deck. It was still foggy, but I could see the edges of the neighbors' yards now. I sat down, trying to force myself to be calm. I opened my Facebook app and scanned the feed: nothing from her recently. But she had posted a photo of the fog-shrouded running trail at 5:42 a.m. "Right when she must have gotten there," I said aloud to Wesley, who was sitting upright at my feet. Lavinia whined, cocking her head at me, seeking some reassurance. I ignored her. If Catherine had posted that photo at 5:42, and was running four miles, she should have been home by now. It wouldn't take her almost an hour and a half to run that distance.

I navigated to Catherine's page on my phone and refreshed. The photo was the most recent post. There were several comments praising the image, and one asking her why she was up so "damn early." None of them had been answered. This meant she had not been on Facebook since those statements had been posted: She always answered comments.

I put on my sweatpants and grabbed my keys, leaving the dogs out on the deck, which we never did when we weren't home. Wesley barked, and I heard him pawing the French doors, confused.

I had left my car in the driveway overnight, and as I was opening the door, one of our neighbors, Richard Copley, jogged past, finishing his own run. He waved without looking at me, distracted by his exhaustion. It was cold, with temperatures in the 20s, but he was wearing running shorts. His only nod to the weather was a thin white long-sleeved technical shirt and a baseball cap.

"Have you seen Catherine?" I yelled at him, noticing his earphones and their thin web line to his iPod.

"What? Sorry..." He pulled the earbuds out. He looked concerned, his eyebrows knitting in worry, not irritation.

"Catherine left to run at her usual time this morning," I panted, as if I'd been sprinting. "But she's not back yet. She's not answering her phone. Have you seen her?"

"No, I—" I started to get in the car when he said, "no," but he kept talking. "Is she running in the neighborhood, or at the river trail?"

"River trail," I called through my opened window as I started to back out of the driveway. He stood in the street.

"I'll keep an eye out for her."

We lived a short distance from the road that led down the steep hill to the river by the Big Dam Bridge parking lot, but there were corners and steep grades. I went as fast as I dared. The trees were brown and bare; they wouldn't begin to bud and leaf for at least another month, when color would explode throughout the city, especially around the Arkansas River that flowed toward the Mississippi Delta. Without fog, I could have seen it, dark and gray, through the naked branches and between the houses propped up on stilts that lined Overlook Road, a steep straight hill that ran down to the river shore parks.

Instantly, I felt relief when I saw her silver Acura parked in one of the first spaces, closest to Rebsamen Road. "She's here. She's here. She's here." I chanted to myself as I approached the lot. I still couldn't see the river, though it was probably less than 20 or 30 yards down the bank, buried in the velvet fog. The little bit of path I could make out was empty, but I heard the footfall of a runner as I got out of the car. I jogged a couple of steps toward the end of the path, where I could see the vague shape of a water fountain, but the runner who emerged, first a shadow, and then a figure, was a man. He turned to cross the parking lot and mount the path to the bridge. He vanished into the clouded morning. I looked down to see I was still wearing my slippers.

● ● ●

And now I know things that only a few other people knew, one whom I despise and blame, and one whom I have now forgiven. I am bound to them because we know these things only we knew, and that is my way of resurrecting the dead, or at least of pretending the dead know I do forgive.

I did know my wife was having an affair; that is what I didn't want to know. I despised her for believing that she was fooling me, and I was humiliated because she was trying to trick me.

Are affairs addictions — a promise of some delicious reward that causes the addict to behave both impulsively and compulsively? Over the course of those months, I saw my wife begin to behave like an addict in many ways, building small secrets into her days, into her routine. She was incrementally more distant, less accessible and less vulnerable to me.

Her other compulsions and impulses also seemed at heightened levels, as if they all rose together from the same deep well. She wasn't saying no to herself, and someone else wasn't saying no to her, either.

Just because I'm a therapist doesn't mean I'm not just as adept as anyone else at avoiding painful realities — or thinking that I can. Once she confessed, I saw the evidence all around me: how much she had spoken of him, his influence on her choices of trivial things — restaurants, what to watch on television — how she broke plans with me with 10 minutes' notice if something came up he needed. I hadn't wanted to see it, and so I didn't. But even at the time, one thing I couldn't avoid was her growing attachment to her iPhone. She looked like the Hollywood starlets I saw on the covers of celebrity magazines in the checkout line at the grocery store, with that technical appendage attached to her palm whatever she was doing, making breakfast, watching television, putting her makeup on.

"Who was the text from?" I had asked her one night, impulsive as well: I spoke as I thought the question. She had asked me to drive home from Cheers in the Heights neighborhood of Little Rock where we'd had a late dinner. I was driving her car so she could check email on her phone, but it buzzed a text alarm almost immediately after we pulled out of the parking lot.

"Work..." she said vaguely, and her self-conscious, assessing sideways glance at me made me skeptical. She clicked a reply, and then toggled back up with her long, deft fingers. I was stopped behind someone turning left off Pine Valley Road, which wound out of the Heights to our neighborhood. I took this road often to avoid Cantrell Road's many traffic lights and regular lane closures. I turned to hear her answer, and I saw her delete the whole message thread.

She was silent. "Why are you deleting all those messages?" I sounded a little frantic when I wanted to sound forceful, or at least hint that I could see something was happening right under my nose.

"What?" she asked, staring into the rectangular white screen that was blazing like the sun in the dark car. I didn't repeat my question. She wasn't listening, or she would have refused to answer. After the driver turned, we traveled a few more curves and hills into Kingwood, our neighborhood between Cantrell Road and the Arkansas River, before she gave up on another response and tucked the phone into her purse, which she held in a miserly way in her lap.

She said nothing and gazed out the window at the passing trees. "That house is for sale?" she said, pointing, but we had passed it.

"Which one?"

"The one that's for sale," she said, and smiled, reaching over to pat my leg with her left hand as I drove, recalling a recurring joke in our 13 years together. I relaxed slightly, but she took her hand away and kept looking out of the car at the houses we drove by. I wanted her hand back.

This is when I first used the magical thinking of a cuckolded husband: *If she puts her hand back on my leg, she's not cheating on me with her boss. If she turns to me at the next four-way stop and starts a conversation, she still loves me. If she still loves me, she is not cheating on me.*

And that is when I knew what I didn't want to know, and I didn't say anything, on the way back from burgers and beers, where she met me after coming from a late meeting. I knew who he was, and it was a painful thing to realize your wife is in love with someone you despise.

• • •

At the bridge, I ran back to Catherine's car. I could see she had done what I had asked her multiple times not to do: She'd thrown a jacket and a shopping bag over her purse and left it on the floor of the passenger seat instead of putting it in the trunk or leaving it at home. The doors were all locked.

I looked around again, but this time I heard nothing, and no one came into view from the fog. It was now almost 7:30 a.m. Something had to be wrong. Catherine was not cavalier about time and getting to work. I went back to my car, thinking I would drive the road that ran parallel to the path and the tree-covered trail on the north side of the street. It was foggy; maybe she'd been hit by a car, or hurt herself running and had to walk back.

Why wouldn't she call? I thought, but silenced myself.

I was nervous, and I pushed the alarm button by mistake on my car's remote, shattering the fog-cushioned silence of the parking lot and jarring me so much I dropped the keys and had to fumble for them while the blaring tones coursed out across the morning. Beyond what I could see, I could hear traffic on the I-430 Bridge about two miles to the west, the white noise of the commute. I didn't have any way of knowing which direction she had gone — north and east over the bridge into North Little Rock and Burns Park? West toward the I-430 Bridge and Two Rivers Park? Or east along Rebsamen Road, where I was preparing to drive.

I pressed the unlock button and got in the car, but I was shaking and had to use two hands to insert the key into the ignition of my Subaru. I backed out, turning on my headlights to bright and scanning everything in my view. I stopped at the turnaround in the parking lot and called her again. Straight to voicemail.

I texted her again: "Where are you?! I'm worried. I cannot find you." I turned on the sound on my phone and set it on the passenger seat. I steered the car down Rebsamen and tried to keep my speed slower than 10 miles per hour.

I found myself caught in a thickening stream of morning commuters to Riverdale offices and to downtown. The driver behind me flashed his lights, impatient with my slow speed. I turned into the first entrance to Murray Park that ran along the Little Rock side of the river, and I scanned the pavilions and tried to see down to the water of the boat launch. I drove through the linked parking lots, switching my lights from bright to normal, never satisfied with what I could see in the fog, which wasn't much. And wasn't Catherine.

I turned left back onto Rebsamen Road and headed again toward downtown among the commuters. I scanned the roadsides, finding nothing. I turned into the second Murray Park entrance, which led to a bigger area, including the dog parks, where we sometimes took

Wesley and Lavinia. The trees were tall and provided shade and some coolness even on the most hot and humid summer days, but now they seemed to hold the fog in their branches and to push it down on the one-lane road that wound around the fencing. Hopeful, I drove the small loop, knowing Catherine liked to run there, watching the dogs playing with their owners in the early morning. There were no dogs now, and no Catherine. I returned to Rebsamen and drove to the golf course. I turned in there and repeated the drill, flashing my brights on and off, scanning the roadside and parking lots. I turned back onto Rebsamen, but when I got to the end of the golf course without finding her or hearing from her, I was too scared to proceed alone.

"9-1-1 operator. What is your emergency?" I didn't remember pushing the numbers.

"My wife. I cannot find my wife," I stuttered. I was still driving the car, aimed back toward the Big Dam Bridge parking lot.

"Where are you, sir? What happened?" asked the operator, with professional calm. Aggravating calm.

"My wife, she went for a four-mile run, at 5:30 a.m., and it's been more than two hours, and she is not home. I'm at the Big Dam Bridge. Her car is here, but I cannot find her."

"Maybe she got a late start? Went farther than planned?" She asked, probing.

"She has to be at work by 8 a.m., or earlier, every day. She's never late. Something has happened to her. Maybe she's hurt and can't get back to her car. Something is wrong!" I heard myself screaming. I stopped in the middle of Rebsamen Road. A driver was honking behind me. I didn't know what to do.

"Where can I send an officer, sir?" the operator asked. Cars were passing me.

"The Big Dam Bridge parking lot," I answered. "I'll be by her silver Acura TL," I instructed, calmed slightly by having to tell someone what to do. "How long will it be? Something is really wrong. I'm sure of it."

• • •

It is an axiom of betrayed women, which they tell me in the therapy chair, that wives know who their husbands will cheat on them with; in fact, they usually know *before* the affair begins, many claim. Who better understands a man than the woman who looks after him, sleeps next to him, responds to his enthusiasms with more of what engages him and moderates her behavior to minimize his indifference? If I were honest, sitting in that chair, I would have to admit I could have predicted this as well, if I had believed before it started that she had the capacity for such betrayal. I know her. I observe her all the hours of the day she allows me to, not only as her husband but also as a trained observer, one with context outside of our marriage, with the knowledge accumulated by several generations of an entire profession. But what I didn't do, which those wives were doing, was modify myself to continue to capture her.

Catherine is competitive and ambitious, and simultaneously very feminine, which masks her hardness and self-interest well and in a way that makes her palatable to ambitious, competitive men, especially here in the South, where conventions are the silent social and psychological taskmasters of even some of the most radical thinkers, the liberal lawyer with the secret affection for the Confederate flag, the upwardly mobile, highly educated woman who won't wear white pants or sandals before Memorial Day. Here live the men who may find women unattractive who are open about their drive or who don't soften their forcefulness as it plays out in front of them, men with the same traits. And I had noticed in our years together that when older, ambitious, competitive men found out she was married to me, 15 years her senior, they wanted to believe that because she liked one older guy, she might like them, too. They could see a window of a chance with her. Sometimes they acted on that perception.

• • •

I drove my car back to the bridge at a crawl, yelling at a driver behind me who honked his horn. More drivers passed me. I did not care. I was still scanning the roadside. As the sun had come up, the fog abated somewhat, or maybe not, maybe I was just used to looking into it. At some points along the way, I could discern the path next to the road, or see a runner, but it was not Catherine. I knew by then I would not find her running. I checked my phone, each time thinking time had passed, and then noticing sometimes less than a minute had. No missed calls. No texts. It was after 8 a.m.

I hoped I would get back to the parking lot and her car would be gone. I imagined going home and being angry with her, telling her I had called 911, and here she was at home, casually getting ready, going in late, for whatever reason, but when I got back to the bridge, her car was still there, untouched.

I sat in my car for 10 minutes, checking my calls, checking Facebook. I got out of the car and began to pace the parking lot.

Every time I heard a runner or saw an inchoate form through the fog, I froze in hope and then wilted when it was not Catherine.

Finally, about 8:25, a black and white car arrived. The officer got out with a notepad and approached Catherine's car, inspecting it. Before I could get to him, he returned to his car and radioed, presumably to run her plates.

"Officer? Officer? I'm her husband. I made the call to 911," I called out when he emerged from his car, and I was almost on top of him. He turned. "You are the husband of..." he checked his notes, "Catherine..." I interrupted him before he could say her last name.

"What did they tell you from 911?" I asked.

"Why don't you tell me what the situation is?" he asked, again. He was very calm. It was like a fork scraping the bottom of a ceramic cup. The nerves in my spine flared, and I made fists to control my frustration.

It's strange to me now to think of those minutes of debilitating fear, because they are infinitely preferable to what came after, the cold, lonely, interminable waiting. Those moments of not knowing meant there was still something to hope for.

I remember so clearly my own search for Catherine up and down the running path, but the stages and processes of the search after that are a blur. There was at first the one officer, and to my surprise, I did not have to do a lot to convince him that Catherine was in danger. Then there was another black and white car, and then there were several. Uniformed officers talked to me, and then a plainclothes detective, from the LRPD Violent Crimes-Missing Persons unit.

He wanted me to come down to the department to go over everything with him if she didn't turn up.

"Now?" I asked, looking around, willing the fog to abate. "I don't want to leave..."

"Not yet," he said. "If she doesn't turn up."

They would keep looking for her, however, of course. A quiet, cautionary mental whisper told me to be careful.

I must have called or texted my friend Chuck, because I remember him being there at the Big Dam Bridge parking lot, holding out coffee for me in a travel mug, and handing me my phone when I couldn't find it. He'd been my friend since high school, but he didn't know about the trouble Catherine and I had had recently, and that was comforting to me, not to have a shadow on her I had to help him navigate. I might have thought because of this secrecy, he wouldn't know enough to give me wise counsel, but attorneys like him seem to prepare for the worst as a routine.

"You've got to have a lawyer to talk to them," he half whispered, half mumbled to me, with his back to the uniformed officers. I was looking out toward the Arkansas River, or where it would be when the fog burned off completely. He was shifting his gaze from my face to the movements of the police behind me.

"I want to help them find her," I protested.

He ignored me. "I'm calling Brooke Borders right now."

"Aren't you an attorney? Can't you be my attorney?"

"I'm not that kind of attorney. I don't do criminal law."

I felt my jaw tense and the nerves light up down into my shoulders and arms. "I'm not a— I don't need—"

"If you're talking to the cops, you do need," he answered, his ear already to his phone. I heard a wordless voice, and he walked down toward the river, speaking with care directly into the phone. I could see the gray-navy of the waves through the dissipating fog finally, and what looked like a deeper, darker color beneath them, that seemed an immobile pool of infinite depth, as if the Arkansas River were just a surface mirage to protect us from the knowledge that there is a deep gash in the world just blocks from our home.

I took a sip of the cooling coffee and saw my hand shaking as I lifted the mug. I had a second of disbelief at what was happening, thinking with longing of the cold quiet morning in the house before Catherine left and didn't return. When she was still there for me to reach out to, to touch.

Chuck handed me the phone.

"I hear you're having a pretty terrible morning, sir?" said a very Southern-accented, girlish voice. I shot Chuck my question with a look.

"She's really good. She's the one you want," he said.

She continued talking after I assented.

"Do you wish to retain me as council?" Chuck, who must have heard her, nodded. I nodded, and then said that I did.

"I will be with you for absolutely any interviews that take place anywhere," she said.

"But I—"

"Yes, I know, you want to help, you want to be part of the solution. Of course. But you are not on the same side as the police. You want to find your wife, and they want to arrest someone. Might as well be you."

"I just can't believe—"

"That's why you have me," she sighed. She was impatient. I could imagine her, a woman whose care and feeding were expensive, with that high, feminine, delicate voice, rolling big blue eyes at her office ceiling. "Never, ever talk to the cops. We can decide together what you'll share with them, but why would you cooperate without an attorney? You're not as smart as you think you are, you know, and you don't know what they know, what they think they know about you, and what they intend to do with it. They can lie to you in the interrogation. You won't know what's real and what isn't, and everything will be lined up against you before you even feel suspected."

"Okay." I didn't feel energy to fight her, but I didn't like her, didn't want her with me, and I wanted her to stop talking.

"Don't give them anything for free. You're innocent, so why provide them with ammunition that will keep them from looking for her?" I could feel a following thought, unspoken, behind her words: *And if you're guilty, why give them help arresting you?*

"Yes, yes," I said. "Yes, okay."

Chuck looked relieved. I handed him back the phone.

"Them's that's closest to her is whut done her in," he said, under his breath. "They don't need to get that in their minds about you. Well, let's face it: It's already there, got to be. We need to get it out of their minds."

• • •

I had first noticed Catherine at a party at Chuck's house not long after my first marriage ended. Catherine was home on spring break from the last semester of an MBA program in Pennsylvania. She was 24. I asked Chuck later how he knew such young "co-eds," and he said she was a friend of a friend, and they had both turned up for cocktails that night. Though Catherine had only known Chuck tangentially when I met her, they became good friends. There was an honest warmth and acceptance about him that appealed to her, and when she chastised him for his messy domestic situations — several marriages ending in divorces that he took the blame for in order to write checks and move on — she said it without judgment, and he took her teasing without injury.

I felt the headiness of her attention when I realized I myself was a divorced 39-year-old, starting to gray, and someone who was on spring break was laughing and leaning toward me with energy and palpable attention as I spoke to her.

"You're called 'Catherine,' then? Not Katie or Cathy?" In these first moments of knowing her, she seemed too diminutive for me to address her so formally. I had asked her to confirm her preference when she said her name as she sipped a gin and tonic by the piano in Chuck's year-round sunporch in his Cammack Village home. The little town within the city of Little Rock had small houses, densely packed into streets known really only to those who lived on them. But inside his house felt spacious, expansive, even.

"No one has ever called me anything but Catherine," she smiled up at me. "My mother was determined not to after my sister Amelia became Amy against Mother's will. Isn't Amy so much worse than Amelia?" She looked around for a place to set her almost empty glass.

"Would you like another drink? Something else?" I asked, though I didn't want to leave her to get it.

"No, I better not. I'm driving." Was she telling me she was here alone?

"Is your sister an Amy? Or an Amelia?"

"Oh, she's a total Amy," she laughed and picked up a copy of *Southern Living*, something Chuck's most-recent wife must have left behind when she moved out. She turned it over, and set the glass on the back, picking it up to see if it left a ring. It was dry. She turned away from this task and up toward me.

"Maybe that's the real problem," I suggested. "Maybe your mom didn't want an Amy for a daughter; your mom wanted an Amelia."

"I think you may have something there, my friend!" Without her glass to hold, she talked more with her hands, aping a classic debate-team point with her right hand as a flourish.

"Oh?" I felt myself growing more flirtatious with each of her responses, the force of her attention, the focus of her wide light-blue eyes.

"They have *never* gotten along, and I'm my mother's favorite. You think this is because I allowed her to make me a Catherine?"

"Perhaps it's because you *are* a Catherine." I stepped closer to her, noticing we were alone in the room now.

"What is it you do, Mr....?"

"I'm a psychotherapist."

"Oh, of course you are," she said in a low voice. "Do you prescribe things?"

"Uh, no," I stuttered. "Sometimes I wish I could. My ex-wife does that; she's a psychiatrist. I've got a Ph.D., not an M.D."

"Ah, no better living through chemistry, then?" She laughed, and punctuated her point again, this time by picking up her glass, raising it to me and then drinking the single swallow that was left. I asked her name.

"Catherine Zrzavy," she answered. Her face was blank, but there was a challenge in the eyes. It checked my impulse to repeat it with exaggerated stuttering over all those consonants. Instead I asked what it meant.

"Red-headed," she said. "ZUR-zah-vee," she tutored me charitably.

"There's some red in there." I studied her strawberry blonde hair.

"There's red inside," she answered, still with that wide, candid gaze. She looked like she was committing every wrinkle, every expression of mine to memory.

I heard Chuck moving through the dining room behind us and into the sunporch to announce a toast. She stepped backward, but kept her eyes fixed on my face.

• • •

Immediately, searches were organized to walk the three directions of the running path that spoked out from the parking lot at the bridge, as well as the mile or so of trail in the trees along the north side of Rebsamen to look for any signs of her, or, of course, I knew, her body. I overheard two officers talking about the possibility of her having been struck by a car in a hit and run.

I returned home with Chuck, and the police came to examine her things, her computer, etc. Her company had to release the passcode to her system and email, which her boss did by phone with a detective standing by on her end of the line, as well.

The uniformed police canvassed the neighborhood, and I saw them talking with Richard's wife on her front sidewalk, she glanced toward our house with frequency, anxiousness.

"I talked to her husband when I was leaving the house this morning," I told Chuck, who was sitting on the couch, watching the investigators. At first he seemed merely distracted by them, but his taut posture and focused looks belied the show he was putting on of being there to support me with rote questions and clichéd comments to "get some rest." We were waiting for Brooke to arrive before we all went to the police department together, and I realized he'd be able to tell her with great detail everything the police had looked at, touched or taken.

"Good, that should help," he said, already thinking of something else. "A good alibi will be the best thing for you."

"I can't believe I have to think about that," I said. My thoughts were fracturing, cracking along lines of worry and guilt of not protecting her, of guilt for thinking about protecting myself when she was obviously hurt somewhere. Where is Catherine?!

Chuck was talking, "...is dating one of my law school buddies. She just defended that Little Rock judge in a bribery case."

"He pled guilty," I reminded him.

"He was guilty," he said. He started talking then about publicity in the case.

"What? What do you mean? Publicity?" My mind went first to our secret, to her lover, Robert.

"If — big if — she doesn't come back soon, isn't found, this is the exact kind of case media love. I mean, Catherine's pretty, she's white, she's successful, and she's all-around appealing," he said. "She disappeared doing something women all over this country do every day in a setting that's going to look great on camera. This is going to play. What do they say? This story has legs."

"Catherine is adorable," I said, agreeing, using a word she hated.

"She's adorable, yes," he said. "How many black women and girls disappear every year in the South alone, and you and I never hear about them?" He looked down at his phone, waiting for something. "This is *People* magazine material. Sorry, but it is. You need an attorney who's tough, and media ready. And pretty." He held his phone up with a picture of Brooke. Blonde, well made-up, very pretty; what I had imagined when I was speaking with her at the bridge. Together-looking. "You want people to want to talk to her, to believe her, for her to represent your wife's voice in this in a comparable way. Brooke is all-Arkansan, too. Knows everybody."

"I'm all-Arkansan," I reminded him, churlish at all the help he thought I needed.

"You don't know shit about the law. If this is a fight, you need someone who likes to fight. She really likes to fight. You don't like to fight."

I shrugged. He turned to his phone.

"You know her from work? Do you work with her?" Chuck did a lot of what I thought of as "backdoor law," taking care of things behind the scenes before they made it to prime time. He worked with many of the major firms in town, and moved among them with ease, but he didn't appear in courtrooms or try cases. He probably knew every lawyer in Little Rock.

"I guess so, but you could say I *really* know her."

"What? Don't— Don't be cagey with me right now."

"She's why my marriage to Bobbi ended — well, *she's* not why. I'm why. She was the straw. Don't share that. We were both married then, or I was for a little while."

This should have made me more comfortable telling everything to Chuck. He was so unabashed about his infidelity, and often managed to stay friends with the wives he had cheated on, but I hadn't cheated on my ex-wife, Sandra, and she could barely stand to talk to me. Maybe it was this idea, that Chuck was somehow more successful than I was in forgiving, in being forgiven, that made me lock down even more. I looked up to answer him, but he was lost in his little white screen.

Without forming the words in my mind, or being aware of any kind of decision-making, like an automaton, I went into our bedroom and collected all of Catherine's journals, going back to her junior high years, put them in a Kroger bag, and walked outside, not sure of what to do with them, just knowing I did not want the police to read them. I hadn't ever gone through them, read any part of them, but it would have been unusual for her to write down nothing about her relationship with Robert, when she wrote routinely, several times a week, wherever she traveled, whatever her mood. I wanted no public record, or any record, of any of that.

Through our back fence was a gate that led down into a ravine and an ad hoc path that skirted the backside of the neighbors' houses, parallel to the street on the ravine side. Everyone's property line went down to the creek, but we all just let that go wild outside our fences, none of us having the desire to tame the woods outside our doors. It was winter, but I could walk along the entire length of our neighborhood almost unseen because the incline was so steep down the hill. Walking just 10 yards down put me below the view of any of the windows, as well as the street.

I went three houses down, to Mrs. Judson's empty ranch house. She spent almost all year somewhere else, Florida in the winter with her sister, and Montana for most of the summer with two of her grown children. None of us knew why she didn't sell the house, but she kept up the payments to the lawn company and the maid service year-round. Her husband had lived in Memphis for years, but they hadn't divorced. Her neighbors knew where the spare key was hidden, and I fished it out of the empty terracotta planter at the corner of her property line and let myself in her backdoor.

I had to hurry — Chuck was in my living room, distracted by or waiting for something, and I was breaking and entering three doors down in order to...what? Hide evidence? I reached up to open a small cupboard high above the stove, took down some crystal vases, shoved the Kroger bag to the back, and then replaced the vases. The house was spotless, the clock ticked. It seemed like Mrs. Judson could round the corner from the dining room at any minute, and yet the silence was singularly that of a home where there was no one but me, a silence I would soon learn well.

On the way back to the house, I had a strange, bifurcated feeling, one I had been unfamiliar with until Catherine's affair, the sensation that I was telling myself something that the rest of me knew wasn't true at all, like my thoughts were waves on the surface of an ocean, whose deep currents moved in the opposite direction. I tried to convince myself that I was just hiding the diaries until I knew what the situation with the police would be, until I could talk to Brooke Borders, lay out my fears for Catherine's privacy, and get her advice on managing that, her thoughts on keeping Robert out of it. If I should — or could.

But as I walked up the steps to my back deck, I knew I wouldn't retrieve those journals, and that I wouldn't talk to anyone about the affair, not even Chuck, who had probably heard and seen some of the most vile admissions of human behavior in Arkansas, confessed by people to get money, reduce awards, make settlements. I was already vaguely suspicious of Robert's involvement, and the shadow of another recent death was darkening my thoughts, and weighing on my hopes that Catherine would return.

• • •

I suppose I idealize the memory of our first meeting now, or maybe it's accurate and helps me forget some of the back and forth and up and down that scrapes and bruises lovers as they become a couple, sometimes failing, and then, for us, succeeding. It wasn't an unbroken line from that moment to our wedding, which wasn't for five more years, to accommodate her MBA and then her Ph.D. There was a lot of tension and a couple of nearly final breakups during her job-hunting process as well. She turned down the job she really wanted to accept her position at UALR, but I assured her that all couples go through these periods of adjustment. I repeated to her what Chuck had told me when I was concerned enough to confide in him about her, about us, about her job conflicts.

"He said it will work out because it has to," I said.

"I'm glad you two have solved that, then." She smiled, but she wasn't bright about it, or energetic. It's hard not to let the impact of her affair tint my recollections of our milestones, but I now recalled a shadow passing through her expression, an acquiescence, where I had previously seen willingness.

Through our years together she hadn't aged, or perhaps I was just conscious of the 15-year age gap, a gap Sandra made much of — directly to me when she had the chance or through friends when she didn't. My hair became grayer than black and my physique seemed to slacken and tilt in increments toward the bodies of my father and grandfather. Her hair, with help, stayed that babyish tint of strawberry blonde, and her exercise routines kept her lithe and taut. When we had first been together, I liked her to wear more modest clothing, to ease silent accusations I felt about cradle-robbing, but as she moved into her thirties, she became less sensitive to that criticism and wore more youthful, fitted clothing, deeper necklines, shorter skirts, tighter jeans. Just five years later, I was struck by how she looked five years younger at 33 than she had at 28. And at the same time I looked every moment of my 48 years.

I also learned that Catherine was not as delicate or adorable as she first seemed. Her athleticism was vibrant and electric under her feminine clothes, easily identifiable as the Heights-informed choices of the well-off establishment in Little Rock, trendy pieces from boutiques and expensive staples from exclusive shops, with key insignia I learned to identify in order to shop for her. But her hair was always a little messier than she liked — she would frown every single time she passed a mirror at its unruliness, even when she kept it cropped short for a period after she got her job at UALR. She stayed thin not because she was disciplined — what she ate was junky and processed — but because she couldn't eat very much at a time due to a never-ending nervous stomach.

Just as she wasn't as delicate as she seemed, neither was she as forthcoming as her wide, open face and soft eyes hinted. She was chatty and authentic, sharing self-deprecating details in disarming ways, like the time she told me as she was moving in that she had never in her life cleaned a bathroom. But she didn't tell me that she had a volatile relationship with money, including being dishonest about credit card bills or large expenditures. Once I started looking more closely into her finances, I got regular bills for things like a $2,000 trench coat or sapphire earrings she had bought online. And I discovered that her recent car purchase had been financed at almost 10 percent for eight years. All she had said to me about that purchase was she was happy with the terms of the deal and loved the car.

Maybe her secrets, her veneer, helped me to continue to feel manly around her — it was a deal we both made in silence, with no overt acknowledgement, unlike our vows, but that held us together even more intricately than our wedding promises. Her femininity made me feel like more of a man until I found out she had castrated me.

• • •

Chuck hadn't missed me. He was doing what he had been when I'd slipped out — toggling among apps on his phone, handling things, and I was sure I wasn't the only problem he was working on. When I walked in the living room, where he had seated his 6-foot, heavily built frame on the small sofa mostly used by our dogs to look out the bay window, he told me he was going to check on something the police might already be investigating.

"Let me handle it," he coaxed when I asked if I should come with him. "You don't need to be dealing with this, but you need to be ready if their investigation goes wrong, and they start looking only at you."

"They'll just want to get someone..."

"Yes," he answered. "Exactly. It's better for you to understand that right up front."

When he left, I saw how easily I had kept something from him, something I could just as easily have shared. Is this how Catherine felt? When she was cheating on me? Or, before the affair, when if she'd confessed her growing friendship with Robert, it might not have blossomed and grown so much in darkness? One moment it doesn't feel as if you are keeping anything from another person — I never felt before any desire or need to confide to Chuck about what had happened — but when he left the house that morning, I was actively lying to him by omission, my closest friend, who was trying to help me find my wife and protect me if the worst came true.

The waves on the surface of my consciousness were telling me it was to protect Catherine, but the currents below stirred with resentment and moved with anger in the deep.

Day Two

2

WHEN I WOKE UP the second day, Catherine's car had been taken from the bridge parking lot as evidence, and two detectives, a man and a woman, came to our house to go through her things while the police were excavating her computer files, emails, text messages — basically, her entire digital history. Brooke had approved this, told me to cooperate.

Of course, Catherine's digital history did not date back to her affair. Her old computers had stayed with the university, and she'd upgraded phones. With her new job came new email and phone accounts and a new laptop, as well. I wondered when they would decide to trace her UALR email, and part of me hoped I would never have to see what she wrote to him. They would find out more than I knew about her if they dug back far enough in time; something else needed to come up before that, something that would lead us to her and away from our past.

As I watched them pack and arrange their harvest, I exhaled as deeply as I could, tired of being distracted by the affair, and yet afraid to think clearly about what had happened to her. I'd had the worst night of my life. I was shocked to be left alone, as I was. Once the police knew I would talk to them only with my attorney, they went into their own procedures and routines. Chuck called my patients to tell them why they were cancelled until further notice and called my referral service to request they cancel everything for at least a week.

We had sat in the living room, drinking scotch until I was nearly tipping over. He let the dogs out and walked me into my room, but I couldn't sleep in there, not that night. He helped me down the steps and made up the waiting room sofa.

"Very comfortable. Everyone wants to sleep in their office," he said, while he tucked the sheets in.

I must have passed out. But around 11 p.m., I was awake again. The silence was deafening, and every signal in my body told me I wasn't going back to sleep — my restless legs, my hyperactive thoughts. I tried not to think of her affair, of the possibility that she had run off with Robert, of her leaving by her own free will. I couldn't ask anyone to check his whereabouts, though I was wild to know. I got up around 1 a.m. and Googled him. His Facebook page was private, but not blocked. His cover photo, changed just days before, showed him and his wife in some Arkansas scenic location, apparently from the holidays, and taken by a professional photographer. The latest news article about him online mentioned an upcoming venture capital deal he was running for the state. He didn't seem like someone about to stay up all night. I went back to the sofa with my iPhone, of course, always attached to me, and Netflix on my iPad. I wished I had her journals now, but I couldn't risk getting them at such an hour.

I would need something to calm me down. I hoped Sandra would hear the news and offer to prescribe me something. I was loath to ask for her help, but I needed it.

• • •

After the trip home from the restaurant that night, Catherine and I walked in the house to let our dogs outside into the small side yard, terraced at the top of the ravine. She picked up her iPhone and started to go out on to the deck, "I'll watch them," she said. Wesley, our corgi, and Lavinia, the German shepherd, were "posh," as Catherine said, and didn't always like to go outside and navigate the deck steps alone, so one of us had to go out and ensure the livestock did their chores.

"Leave your phone," I said, looking her in the face. She shrugged and slipped it casually back into her purse and smiled. "You work too much," I explained, but the tightness of her smile didn't welcome more commentary. She kept her mouth fixed, slipped off her work shoes, and stepped into her garden shoes as she followed the dogs outside.

I walked toward her purse, stopped and stared at the side pocket with the phone. It gave the little two-staccato-beats vibration signaling a received text just as I approached. Tucked against a metal grommet, the vibration was louder, a ghost's rattle in a dark room. I stood there, waiting for another notification. I picked up the purse and her briefcase — heavy with her laptop and multiple report drafts nearly spilling out of it — and carried them both toward our bedroom, stopping in her den on the way to set them down in the leather chair where she dumped them when she got home from the university.

I closed the door and waited. I thought I was waiting for the dogs to return and Catherine to come in and start getting them ready for the night. But I was waiting for her to tell me — for someone else to make me know.

Catherine's tenure-line assistant professor of management position at the University of Arkansas at Little Rock looked very tidy to our friends and her colleagues, almost cliché: Arkansas girl makes good and comes home to stay. She was an *Arkansas Times* Academic All-Star, and like other members of the honors program at Little Rock Central, she attended premier colleges and graduate programs, Rhodes, Wharton, Temple. Of course, Robert was assistant dean of the school of business, and his role in her life was not part of the cliché, or perhaps it was the biggest part of the cliché.

But as I saw in the wake of her affair, and the violent aftermath, it was not neat; the nuances were painful and humiliating. The memories of the argument we had when she was trying to decide between the job at UALR and a position at LSU are integrated into the happiest memories I have of her. Her disappointment is intertwined with her love for me.

"Why can't you be a therapist in Baton Rouge, or even New Orleans? Or somewhere in the area?" she asked, after she had gone on seven interviews the spring she defended her dissertation and gotten the two offers. The Louisiana job had a lighter teaching load, higher pay and more demanding research and publishing expectations for promotion and tenure.

We were at dinner in a West Little Rock restaurant — it was Gypsy's then, but by the time she disappeared, it had changed hands — and her usually fresh, pale complexion was blued with flight exhaustion and job-interview stress. Our argument was energetic, but subdued, controlled.

"I've built a practice over my whole career," I explained, again. "I'd have to try to buy into a practice there, and have *bosses*, or hang out a shingle and go a year with maybe two clients before things tipped, if they ever did. I'm 43. I'm at the middle of my career — a switch now could be, well, deadly."

"I'm at the beginning of mine." She would not look at me. Her hand shook as she picked up her martini, but she steadied it and took a prolonged sip. "Besides, you started fresh when you split up with Sandra."

"Exactly," I insisted, deciding to dodge her pointed barb. I was not going to get into an argument over something else: That would be a rookie mistake. "It only worked because I brought a lot of clients with me. I can't do that in Baton Rouge. You can make UALR work. You can start there and advance. If I move now, I'm starting over again, just as I am really seeing things gel. I don't want to be 28 in my career again."

Her eyebrows knitted together and her mouth became very small.

"I'll never have the chances in Arkansas I could have with LSU as a foundation," she said. She looked around the restaurant as if she were identifying the exits. "You want me to limit myself, so you don't have to push yourself."

"Let's unpack what you just said." I sat back in my chair and looked at her, conscious that this was a tactic I had used earlier in the afternoon with a borderline personality patient.

"Unpack it?" Catherine scoffed. "Unpack it." She put down her drink and started to push her arms into her cardigan sweater that was hung over the back of her chair. "Unpack this, my friend..." I remembered our first meeting, when that address had been part of the charm that had moved me closer to her. It chilled me now. "I'm not at fault just because I want something that opposes your interests, your stability. I cannot believe you won't even consider this move, won't even talk about it hypothetically." She grabbed her purse and slung it over her shoulder.

"You want me to settle because you're afraid. That's what I'm 'unpacking' right now."

She had stood up then, and walked out of the restaurant on Rodney Parham and had somehow gotten to her friend's house in Hillcrest to stay the night. We'd been married three months.

She came home the next morning and said she would take the UALR job. I tried to talk to her more about it, but she would only say she was finished "unpacking it," and made the call to accept the offer. She went outside to call LSU. I did not use that phrase around her again.

• • •

Her iPhone was missing along with her. Though they had pinged the phone to try to physically locate her, nothing had come up, and Chuck, who had returned later with Brooke Borders herself, surmised that whoever had caused this to happen had taken the phone apart and destroyed it.

"I'm sorry," he said when he saw my face.

"It's just... so... so chilling," I confided. That was the first time I gave in to my hysteria, and I sat down on the ottoman I was standing near and began to hyperventilate. When I became aware of my surroundings again, I was lying sideways on the floor, my hands over my face, heaving from trying to breathe. Lavinia was sitting next to me with her paw resting on my hip, her big black eyes stoically fixed on me.

Brooke was seated on the sofa. She was looking through a file of papers she was holding in her lap, trying not to look at me. She seemed used to being perfectly self-contained. I was embarrassed and rose too quickly, making myself dizzy, seeing little points of light that wafted up and out of my view, but her face gave away no reaction. She was blonde, but not what I had pictured or had seemed to see in Chuck's dim cellphone photo, a light, soft almost-white blonde, as if she were bleached every day in some Disney-fied kind-hearted sun, not the harsh wiry blonde of a Barbie. Her hair was shoulder-length and wavy, and her narrow, intent face was freckled. She was small, and looked like Tinker Bell. My concerns about her involvement resurfaced as Chuck lurched in from the kitchen with a cup of coffee in one hand and a glass of water in the other.

"Are you ready to go talk to the police? Detective Greene is waiting," she said. Her posture was focused, waiting to be sprung. She was eager.

"Are you...hungover?" Chuck asked in the practiced way of someone who asks people things no one else is willing to. He was sitting across the room with the coffee he'd made us that morning.

"I'm not hungover," I said, though that was a lie. I was dehydrated and my head was pounding. "I haven't slept."

"Of course, you haven't," Brooke said.

"You're not going to feel better any time soon, unless they find her perfectly okay," said Chuck.

"Yes," I said, sitting up, resting my back against the chair. Lavinia lay down, resting her head on my foot.

"I mean, you're going to feel bad until you get used to feeling bad, and that's the best you have to hope for," he pushed on.

"Thanks for the therapy," I said, grim, knowing he was right. I could feel the anxiety, grief and frustration settling into my bones. It felt like a cellular malaise — like I was getting a cold, so tired inside my muscle, my tissue — but more energized and biting, as if my insides were sharp and would cut me to shreds from within.

"We all need friends," he said firmly, draining the mug and setting it down on the end table. I thought how Catherine would be irritated that he didn't use a coaster. I stood up and picked one up off the coffee table on my way across the room to him, and put it under the glass.

"She will not want to see a ring on the table when she gets back," he said, patting my arm. I knew it cost him to say such an optimistic thing. We walked out to Brooke's car, a black Tahoe, and I got in the back seat, still dizzy.

· · ·

I became more interested in her work, her colleagues, once Catherine started at UALR, in the university and her program. The next day, between patients at my office, I Googled, clicking down leads of what her life would be like on the faculty there, what this position might mean for both of us — her commute, her campus, her colleagues, her programs. I had lived in Little Rock off and on my entire life, but the university, on a spreading campus south of I-630, was out of my routine and my circle of friends. I was more familiar with Hendrix, a private liberal arts college in Conway, 30 miles away, where I sometimes lectured for seminars, than this large state university in my own city.

This must have been the first time I saw him, or a photo of him: Dr. Robert Gewinn, assistant dean of the School of Business. I am not sure how I got on his page — he wasn't in the management faculty, which she was joining, but I must have been searching through the administration, up the chain of those who had made the decision to hire her.

And even then, before I met him, or had even heard his name from her, when I saw his photo, I remember thinking, *Oh, he is the kind of man who will like Catherine,* but I wasn't worried, just happy I wanted my beautiful, brilliant, secretly secretive wife to be liked and valued at the job I had pushed her to accept. So I wanted it, too, and I wanted things to go smoothly there for her so I wouldn't have to answer for my own decisions. Now I see I was just like those wives who know who their husbands will cheat on them with, even though I didn't know it then. I knew nothing of what would happen over the course of her career at UALR, with him, or what the disaster of his family life would do to my own marriage, and to my wife.

• • •

After she backed out of my driveway and started down Kingwood to Pine Valley Road, Brooke got to work.

"We don't have a lot of time from here to the station. Chuck picked up a nice piece of information this morning already," she said, handing the conversation off to him.

"They told *you*?" I was confused.

"Chuck finds things out," she said with a small uptick at the corners of her mouth. "That's what connections are for."

He turned his bulky frame toward me. "Your neighbor, Rick?"

"Richard."

"Richard, your neighbor, said he saw you leaving, frantic, looking for Catherine."

"So, that's an alibi?" I hurried along the story, eager to get to the search for her.

"It helps," Brooke corrected me. "Of course, you could have staged that." She watched my frustrated shrug in her rearview mirror.

"And," Chuck stressed, shooting Brooke a similar annoyed glance, "Richard saw you out back with your dogs when he left for his run, about twenty minutes after Catherine left."

Brooke was silent.

"But they've already got initial cellphone records pulled," said Chuck, and I could tell from the way he leaned toward me, even though it was unnatural and uncomfortable, the way his eyes met mine, that this was going to be good news. "She pings towers consistent with her being at the Bridge, lining up with when you said she left, data stuff, Facebook, that kind of thing. You ping towers around your house the entire time."

"They're not that far apart," I said.

"You guys have different carriers," he said, his only explanation.

"The whole time? I wasn't on my phone that early," I said.

"You were using data, reading online? Email? Location services backing up, stuff like that. And then it explodes when you start to try to find her. The phone puts you at the house pretty much the whole time." He slapped Brooke's arm, triumphant in even this small win. She didn't respond to him. We were getting to the Heights. Pine Valley had turned to Kavanaugh. She was taking neighborhood roads, avoiding Cantrell so far.

"Couldn't I have gone down, found her, hurt her—" I couldn't say murdered — "and then come home?" I asked to cut Brooke off. I couldn't stand to hear her voice, her version of the evidence, a version in which I had hurt my wife.

"No. No, because Richard saw you outside with the dogs only twenty minutes after Catherine left, and your data pings are frequent enough to put you here too much to have left the house."

"Of course, those cellphone tower records can be bullshit," said Brooke. "But I'm not going to fight them if they're using that ridiculousness in our favor."

"Right!" said Chuck, looking back at me.

"What do you mean, 'bullshit'?" I asked.

"They're pretty meaningless to pinpoint someone's whereabouts with any real local accuracy," Brooke said. "They could prove you weren't in Chicago, but were in Memphis, that kind of thing, but..."

"There's tower overlap, ambiguity over which tower relays the call, the caller's or the receiver's," finished Chuck.

"I'm okay with all of it if they're not using it against you," Brooke said, looking at Chuck instead of me. "To me it means they have some reason not to suspect you...specifically."

Chuck agreed and told me without police attention I could focus on finding Catherine. "You won't have this terrible distraction," he said.

"I could have done it another time, right?" Why was I so able to imagine planning this? Why was I pushing this point? Brooke watched me through the rearview, still expressionless, as if her makeup were a mask. We turned onto Cantrell at the light on Kavanaugh.

"Also, no!" Chuck pulled his seat belt out as he leaned farther toward me. "A cyclist saw Catherine arrive at the Bridge lot. Alone."

I unfastened my seatbelt. "Someone saw her?" I felt nauseated by intense emotion. She had lived after I had seen her; maybe she had spoken after her fog comment fell out of the air around me as she left. "Did she say anything? What did they say?"

"They didn't talk." He patted my leg, looking away from me. "The guy was on a bike."

"In this weather?" Brooke remarked.

"—so he didn't stop," Chuck continued, also ruffled by her cold distraction, her impassive conversation. "But he saw her, he knows her — not by name, but by sight. All those cyclists, runners start to recognize each other. She went down there a lot? Early like that?"

"She had started to," I said. "In the past year."

"Yeah, he just knew her because he rides that time of day, and sees her there, too. They're looking for other people like him, but this is enough, for now."

"They'd have to go pretty far to construct this as a crime you could have committed," said Brooke. Her dark pink lipstick made her mouth look plastic. "That doesn't mean they won't, so don't relax. Like I said before, we don't know everything they know, or what they think they know about you."

She stopped at the light on Riverfront and Cantrell. I looked over to the tracks where I remembered Robert's son had died in a car-train collision last year.

"Is there anything I should know? Anything they'll find that will make them think you might have been involved?"

"No." I said.

"Let me just tell you straight, again; you're a therapist, right? So, you know what it's like to tell people things they don't want to hear, but that they need to know, that they need to really get because they *need* to behave in a certain way."

"Okay."

Brooke held my gaze from the rearview mirror. "Do not talk to the cops alone. Do not talk to the cops with me unless I say you should say something. It's up to the state to prove anything. Your only defense is silence."

"I really... I don't feel I need a defense. Especially not now."

"Don't talk to the cops if you're innocent. Don't talk to the cops if they can prove you're not. These are the rules for you, got them?"

I said I understood, but I thought of the journals and my small, growing secrets and wasn't sure which category I was falling into.

At the precinct, Chuck took the car to run some errands, and Brooke and I were welcomed by Detective Schmidt, whom I recognized from TV news reports on other missing persons cases. I could see the media coverage starting to play out in my imagination, and my nausea intensified.

He sat across from Brooke and me in the interview room, 40s, white, a shaved head that hid his balding pattern from all but close inspection. He was about Chuck's size and had the pallor of those who eat too much Waffle House, which was emphasized by the fluorescent lights in the station.

He started to talk to me about the timeline. Before I answered anything, I looked to Brooke. She would either give me a quick nod to indicate an answer, which I kept brief, or she wouldn't do anything, and I would say that I didn't know. That only happened once, when he asked if I knew of anyone who would hurt Catherine.

"You don't know, or you don't want to say?" He said, casting a side-eye to Brooke.

"Bill," she said.

"Brooke," he answered, aping her.

"I don't know."

"Look, just because you have trouble in your marriage, and you tell me about it doesn't mean you did something to her. Everybody's got marriage troubles," he said, shooting a jibing look at Brooke. I felt my blood start thumping in my ears, drowning him out. I didn't hear his next words exactly, but understood that it also wouldn't have to be public, at least not now, not while they looked for her.

"You should be looking for her right now," Brooke said. "And I haven't heard him tell you there were any troubles. Don't bait the guy — or me. Jesus." He faced off her withering look. I suspected this was part of her courtroom persona, her emotions on tap for performances. She hadn't been this concerned about me in the car, or anywhere else.

"You don't know what we're doing, counselor," he said to her.

"That's the issue, isn't it?" she asked.

"You got anything you want to tell me?" he asked me. How many times would I be asked that today? My answer became more entrenched, more believable even to me. I didn't look at Brooke to know I could give it to him.

"No."

• • •

After the affair ended, I learned that Robert's son, Tyler, who had been briefly employed at UALR in an outreach office, was probably the first of all of us to know, or at least to confront Robert with suspicions. He had seen them together in one of the coffee shops or dining areas on campus and had asked his father why he was with this young new hire so much, indicating he had noticed them together more than once. Robert hadn't spoken to Catherine or answered her emails, phone calls or texts for a week after he had reported the conversation with Tyler to her during a walk down the hall between their respective office suites. When she moved to follow him into his office, he whispered, "Do not follow me in there," and walked on, shutting the door behind him. Through the glass, she watched him smile obligingly to his secretary in the dean's suite, pick up a message, tap something on the table and raise his eyebrows inquisitively toward the secretary, who answered something Catherine could not hear.

She loved him.

She loved a man who could treat her like he loved her until someone confronted him, and then he could order her to stand in a hallway as he tried to walk out of her life to rejoin his day, and check up on some trivial matter with his assistant as if Catherine were not standing there, waiting only for him to turn and see her.

This continues to be a conundrum of my own feelings: Of course, I hated him for being part of some of the worst pain of my life, my lowest moments and months as a man. But I also hated him for hurting her, and I would often see those feelings ceding to my anger at her for loving someone who would do that and betraying me when I was the best I could be for her.

But these feelings are cliché, and anyone who has had a friend who's suffered this kind of betrayal is familiar with them, has heard these words before. But it is a particular kind of grief to hate a person for hurting someone who has hurt you so monstrously — and to still love her and want to save her.

• • •

Catherine's sister, Amy, had called within the first 48 hours. She was her only immediate family, but they hadn't been close, Amy being an "Amy" and not an "Amelia." Their mother had died of cancer before our relationship had gotten serious enough for me to meet her, and their father was in a nursing home, oblivious with Alzheimer's. Amy lived in Memphis, and every time she called, she renewed her offer to come to stay, to help search, to wait.

But it didn't feel like an offer; it felt like another sentence, someone to take care of when I couldn't keep my own thoughts in order. And I was not in any kind of care-taking mode.

"It's better if you don't stay here," I finally said in her third call in 24 hours. "The investigators are in and out, and I'm trying to keep everything the way it was; I don't know what will help them find her."

Sighing, she said she would wait, maybe find a friend to stay with. I started to screen calls, letting her and other offers of "help" go to voicemail.

After returning from the precinct, I gratefully abandoned the need I'd felt that day to stay sober. Even one night of no sleep had been excruciating, and I was happy to pour a scotch. Chuck watched without judgment and asked if I shouldn't eat something, too.

"I'm not hungry," I said. I couldn't think of anything I wanted to eat. I'd had some GoLean that morning, Catherine's cereal of choice. But my stomach had roiled in revolt as much then as it did now, just thinking of food.

I hadn't heard from my ex-wife yet, but she had to know about it, living in Little Rock. I knew she would make some kind of contact, though, and the expectation of that weight felt like the heaviness in the air before an ugly storm. I did intend to make use of her by requesting samples or a prescription from her for something that would calm me down, help me sleep.

Having Chuck there helped, and even within 36 hours, I found myself adjusting, somewhat, to this new situation — mainly by self-medicating. I probably drank more in the last day and a half than I had all month. My appointments were cancelled indefinitely, and I made what was requested available to the police, with Brooke's approval, took care of the dogs, and cooked, cleaning up after each meal as thoroughly as I could.

• • •

I don't have the best memory of what I learned and when, things she had told me, things I learned later but then remembered her telling me, or things that I only imagined that turned into memories, because I was drunk, overtired, sleep-deprived, and later on, drugged. I learned things then that I recalled later but had no source for, facts of her life that became the weather around me, realities that just existed, even though I couldn't remember how they came into my mind, whether they really were facts, or her surmisings or her wishes.

For example, I have the idea that when the end came for them, it came quickly. But how, I do not know. They returned to their affair a week after his dismissal of her in the hallway, but I don't know how, and it continued for several months, though they were more careful of his son, and everyone else, after that. Tyler was more aware of them, as well, and more problematic. The end was inevitable; if she had only asked me, I could have told her: "You'll be the loser. You're the professor, the woman, the pariah, and even with tenure, he's the rich, well-connected darling of not only the administration but the state government, as well." I've dealt with this in my practice so many times. But, of course, she didn't ask me.

And then, one Tuesday, on a beautiful though cold January afternoon, I got a call from her. Finding myself with a free afternoon after a patient cancellation, I was out riding my bike on the Little Rock and North Little Rock river trails when her ringtone interrupted my music. I clicked my earbud controls to answer it, and she said in a raw, urgent voice that she had something to tell me when I got home; she was leaving early to do so. My stomach started to twist into a little knot near the skateboard park in North Little Rock. She wouldn't leave work early for anything trivial, and certainly not for good news.

"What is it?" I asked her.

"Just ride straight home right away," she said. "I'll be there."

"You'll be there when I get home?" I clarified. "What time are you leaving?"

She said she'd see me soon, and my cell line went dead.

I had to pedal back over the Big Dam Bridge and then up the steep hill to our neighborhood, and for an amateur cyclist like me, it was taxing, but I was powered by my dread and fear. Winter in Little Rock is shades of silver and grey, with little ice or snow that sticks around, and as I rode, the grayness became heavier and more oppressive, an endless shadow of something looming. I tried not to think of what it could be, but fear of her leaving me was so present, I was afraid I would see her loading her car when I finally got to our house on Kingwood Road 45 minutes later.

When I walked in, Catherine was in the kitchen with the dogs. I clicked in from the garage, my bike clips scraping the wood flooring, and she stood up and demanded that the dogs go outside. Lavinia, our older dog, smallish for a German shepherd, was clingy and didn't want to leave us.

"Lavinia, go outside!" I said, more stern than I meant to be. She slunk out the door Catherine had opened but stood on the deck with her nose to the door. I closed the blinds over her pleading face. Wesley, our 2-year-old corgi, was oblivious and followed the sun to bathe in any warmth he could find.

I took off my bicycle shoes, and Catherine sat down again in the kitchen chair nearest the window. I saw that she had dropped her bags around her on the floor when she had arrived home. She still had her coat on. It was the Burberry raincoat I got her in England when I was away at a conference. The thought flew through my mind, "Was she with him when I was in London?"

I knew what she was going to say, but I didn't know how it would end, what she would say next, what it would lead to, what I would say, what I would give her as an ultimatum, what she would demand of me. I was usually a man with ready scripts, prompts and interpersonal tactics. I wanted to step outside this kitchen and be my own therapist, give myself advice, but I couldn't quiet my mind. That loss of control, that feeling of a spinning, wheeling, wild situation hadn't completely dissipated after that day.

"I have something to tell you, and it's time I did. I have treated you badly. I have lied to you too much—"

"Is it Robert?" I interrupted her.

"Yes," she said, emphatically, yet quietly.

I looked at her, searching her face. I mustered all the energy I had, to act as if I weren't already completely sure of what was coming in answer to my next question. I wanted to experience all the shock and hurt that were coming to me.

"Did you sleep with him?" I asked. In my head I sounded strident, demanding, outraged. But when I heard it, it was breaking, broken sounding. I looked down. I heard Lavinia whining outside.

Then Lavinia was quiet, and there was silence. I didn't want to look in her face, but the silence persisted, and reflexively I glanced up. My heart made its own painful squeeze, because Catherine's expression was pressed, pained, but her eyes were on the door to the deck where she could see the dog, brown in the gray and brown day, concerned and waiting.

When she looked back at me, she met my eyes and tilted her head, as if to say, "Of course." And though I knew she must have been with him, having that vague understanding that she was in love with someone else, I had somehow told myself that even if she fell for another man, she would-not-would-not-would-not sleep with him. And when she moved her head that half inch in acquiescence, I had to confront the thing that I had told myself had not happened. Because by telling myself that, I could continue to believe in the two of us, inviolate.

In that small movement, that unexpected expression on her face of "What else would I have done?" I became a kind of raw man, turned inside out. I started to wilt into my chair, after having what I thought was a somewhat aggressive posture, with my shoulders up and back, my chest open and directed toward her, my feet firmly planted. The momentum of the slight falling forward, though, kept me going, and I didn't care, didn't try to stop myself.

"Oh, my darling! You're falling..." she whispered, hoarse, and somehow she met me on the floor, was there before I was, pulling me into her arms. My weight pushed her against the kitchen wall, and the framed photos from a trip we took to Big Sur rattled a moment after the thud. I could hear a yelp from Lavinia on the deck. I didn't cry. I just smelled my wife's neck, hoping there would be nothing sensuous to tell me she had touched him today, that he had kissed her or said something close to her ear. If I were Lavinia or Wesley, I could have smelled it on her, all along. They probably had.

We lay there on the floor, me practically crushing her. I felt her chest fall after she exhaled, and she said, "It's over now."

I lay there, then, feeling that she was lifting me up and letting me down with her breath. I had turned and my back was toward her, my shoulder crooked uncomfortably under her face. I could no longer see her, but I could smell her, the scent of her day, her faded Shalimar, such a strange "old lady" perfume for a young woman, on her arm wrapped around me, resting under my chin, coffee, a little sweat from wearing her coat in her warm car on the way from the university and sitting in it at the table. *I am like a dog; scent is my primary sense. I can smell her whole day.* But I didn't know what Robert smelled like, what innocuous note among her scents could be a souvenir of him.

"I don't know if you'll want me, but I want to stay and find out. I'll leave if you tell me to," she said. "I'll do what you want, but I want to stay." I didn't get to feel good about her saying this because I resented so much that she had had the opportunity to plan what she would say to me when I felt ambushed, surprised into wordlessness. The control I had lost, she was asserting.

I continued to lie there, trying to feel every cell in my skin that was touching her body, not wanting to get up and go into the evening that was ahead of us, not wanting to turn and face her.

"I'm sorry," she whispered. "Please. I am so sorry."

The recollection of this moment is as awful as the living of it was then. And yet I couldn't stop thinking of it because it is one of the most alive, intimate and vibrant, though horrible, memories I have of us together in those last few years.

• • •

Only after she disappeared did I remember the strange evening we'd had after she told me. We went out that night to a fundraiser she'd been given tickets to at work, tickets Robert couldn't use. My shock still rendered me an automaton, and all I could think of was that we had the tickets, we had our formal wear, we had RSVP'd, and plans were plans. I bullied Catherine into it and felt good telling her what to do, forcing her to say yes to me when I knew she wouldn't dare say no.

We got ready in silence. I went to my closet and extracted the pieces and parts of my formal wear, while she stood in front of the sink in the guest room, reapplying makeup and curling her hair in her black slip. When I was dressed with my cufflinks, bow tie and patent shoes, I walked out to the garage and backed the car out, letting it idle in the driveway for five minutes or so, and then I turned off the engine. I felt the seductive chill of the righteously angry, and I wanted it to last.

She didn't talk at all in the car on the way downtown except to ask me once if I was sure I wanted to go, if I felt all right to be around people. I didn't answer her. I just kept staring forward at the road.

I had never been to this gala before, or to many others. The tuxedo had been a gift from Catherine when she started to be asked to things to represent the School of Business, probably by and for (and sometimes with) Robert, and walking into the arrivals hall at the Statehouse Convention Center from the cold walk from the car made me regret my decision. The conversations mingled together on this level and the next, which we could see up the escalators filled with ball gowns of every color and punctuated with black tuxedos like mine, to form a suffocating roar of sound that obliterated anyone talking around me. As we walked toward the table to check in, I realized I might have made a frightening error.

"Is he going to be here?" I asked, grabbing her elbow as she strode ahead of me to put our names in.

She tottered a little on her heels and looked down as she tried to steady herself, not leaning against me, I noticed, but putting her hand out to counterbalance her fall.

"No. I wouldn't—" she saw my eye contact and knew I was challenging anything she might attest that she wouldn't do morally would not be believable now. "No. A donor bought a table, and I — we," she looked at me to dispel the obvious question about the pronoun, "were encouraged to come."

By Robert.

We rode the escalator up into the roar to mingle and gaze without comprehension at all the silent auction's offerings. As Catherine leaned over to write her name and our bidding number on a Hot Springs weekend getaway, I kept up the slow pace through the throng.

I remember this coldness of mine, pushing myself into the tuxedo-clad and red, navy, black, white and gold formal-gown-wearing crowd in that ice-white hall to get away from her, to leave her behind. I did not wait for her, and after just a few moments, she was covered by the waves of gala attendees and disappeared.

Day Three

3

I SAID I WOULD BE FINE on my own after Chuck left, but I was antsy and feeling stir-crazy. I woke reflexively at 5 a.m., when Catherine would get up to her alarm to run or work out. That morning, jangly with the isolation, I decided to take the dogs for a walk in the neighborhood.

Again, I hadn't slept, and even with a heavy hangover, I wanted to move around, to leave the house. I was feeling alone — lonely — missing Catherine. And just since hiding her journals, I missed her in a new way. I felt a strange camaraderie with her, one secretkeeper to another.

I knew there had been press coverage, though I was trying to avoid the television news and the internet. Brooke had kept the reporters from my house by coordinating regular updates with the police and letting assignment editors know I was not a person of interest. Chuck had probably had a lot to do with this, too. And, for now, Catherine was merely "missing." I had read the *Democrat-Gazette* story the day before, and I wondered what the local media would make of this vanished Little Rock woman, so I had felt very cautious about going out. But it was still dark when I got outside with Wesley and Lavinia on their blue and red leashes. This was the time of day Catherine had left three days ago. I began walking toward the River Trail.

The three of us made our way down Kingwood toward Beltwood with only the streetlights to show the way. The dogs were restless, too, and eager to be outside the confines of the house with me. I had often walked them while Catherine was running. I was more of a cyclist, a very occasional cyclist, only riding on the weekends or on pleasant appointment-free afternoons. I would never bike on a morning like this, a clear sky over a cold predawn dark. I had on my heavier winter jacket with a sweatshirt underneath, and a scarf with gloves. It had not been this cold three days ago for Catherine.

I followed the street to the three-way stop at the top of the hill down to the river. The neighborhood was silent except for a distant car turning out of a driveway, and some dogs barking at deer or a coyote across the ravine to the north. The dogs made to continue left onto Overlook, as we usually did to make a short, scenic loop of the neighborhood without much traffic, but I pulled them across the street, and we hugged the embankment as we walked toward the intersection with the road that went down, down, down to the River Trail. The sky wasn't even thinking of turning pink to blue yet, and the streetlights, and the bridge and dam lights below them, shone as small bruises of light in the night over the ridge, over the water. I wasn't cognizant of making the decision to walk that direction, but I knew when I left the house that I meant to take the dogs along the route Catherine would have driven to the river.

At the end of the street, I carefully navigated the steep hill before the stop sign that I usually avoided in my cycling routes, while Wesley pulled on the leash, giving himself over to gravity.

"Whoa! Boy-oh!" I called out, afraid he would pull me down, and when I saw headlights coming from my left, headed down the hill, I jerked him back, hard, worried the driver wouldn't see him there on the side of the road. The car was expensively quiet, moving through the winter streets. Here, there was virtually no shoulder. Wesley yelped, mostly in shock, and retreated to stand at my feet while the car, a two-door silver Mercedes convertible, passed us, heading to Rebsamen Park Road below the hill.

I thought of turning back then, worried about walking on the narrow road in the dark with the dogs without any of my reflective clothing on, but I knew I would end up down at the bridge that day at some point. The pull was very strong to go back when I wasn't panicking and could think through my memories of that morning. Maybe something would give me some insight or help me remember anything, any additional detail. And I just wanted to be there, where she had been, in some peace before the day, before the phone began ringing and things had to be done and said to police and detectives, and friends and family.

The walk down the hill took more time than I thought, having only driven it or ridden my bicycle down before, and it occurred to me I would have to walk the dogs back up at some point, which would probably be daylight, and maybe even rush hour, when I would be recognized by our neighbors. But I kept going, and as I reached the fork on Overlook to go left to the Big Dam Bridge or right to Murray Park and Riverdale, I found that, though it was still dark, I could start to imagine the dawn.

• • •

Catherine went to work the Monday following her confession, but she lingered longer over coffee before she left. She went to teach her classes and returned home immediately after they were over. After my last patient of the day left, she came downstairs into my office, tapping lightly on the door.

"May I come in and talk some things over?" she asked. There was a new timidity in her rounded shoulders and downward gaze. I gestured to the chair next to my desk, feeling morally evolved because I didn't make her sit in my patients' chairs as a subject of my examination, humiliated.

"I've decided to leave the university," she said.

I put away the last of my patient files for the day. She returned my silence and waited for me to finish my work, or to respond.

I walked back to my desk from the file cabinet and asked her, "Did he fire you? Or 'strongly suggest' your leaving?"

"No, no. He wouldn't. I mean—" she corrected herself, knowing her familiarity and defense of him would sting. "I mean," she stopped to consider exactly how to word her response. "Whatever *he* would do, he *cannot* suggest I leave, or fire me, because that would expose the university to a law suit."

"Did you talk to him today?" I asked, interrupting her explanation.

"I...I," and when she looked me in the eye to answer, I knew she had. She gathered herself, and said, meeting my eyes, and very calmly, with an even tone, "I told him Friday what I was going to do, and today I told him that I had told you about the affair, and that I am going to leave the university."

Her poise hurt me, and I searched her face and expression. I liked seeing her broken, breaking — it was her regret made manifest. Maybe she wasn't timid, just resigned to the consequences of her actions. I could feel the anger roiling within me and had so far kept her at a cold distance so that I wouldn't experience it as fully as I was afraid it would be. And in that split second, when she addressed me in that way, I was disappointed — and I also felt admiration for her. It occurred to me that I could rely on her to get us through this; beneath this beleaguered patina, there was something so strong in her, so resilient, so unbroken.

"Has he told Petra?" I asked.

"She knows."

"Does she know everything?" I asked, trying to figure out why she had to tell her lover that her husband was now in on the secret. I could feel myself fixating on this bit of information, sleuthing this out.

"I don't know what you mean," she responded, standing up, and then sitting down, smoothing her gray skirt with absent and compulsive gestures. "What 'everything'?"

"That you slept together? I mean, that's what makes it an affair, right? That you fucked him?"

She looked up, directly into my crudeness, and she pushed back her strawberry-blonde hair to fully expose her face to me. She was bold now, or the replica of boldness.

"I don't think she knows the details," she replied softly.

"The details?" I stood over her, my anger finally boiled over, yelling down into her upturned face. She kept it lifted up to me, even though she was flinching under the weight of my yelling. "The details! The details! These aren't details, unless you're a whore..." I saw that I had overshot, leapt too far at once when she blanched at the word. I'd had so many thoughts in response to her I hadn't said aloud, and this one exploded on my lips before I could work up to it. She recovered, though. She steadied herself.

"I'm not a whore," she corrected me. "Whores are paid." She looked down then, and I could only see the top of her head, her hair trailing down her back, the sides falling forward. I could see the shadows of her natural color, an adult's dishwater blonde, along the roots of her part.

"You weren't paid? Is that what you think?" She didn't move or speak. Her hands were now still on her lap.

I thought through some of the appointments she'd gotten on university committees, appointments that were at Robert's discretion. The release time she'd gotten to work on that special research project for the dean's office, also probably Robert's decision, the academic team that worked with the entrepreneurial program at the University of Arkansas, with much success and fanfare when they helped make a nanoscience patent marketable. I was sure there were other things I didn't know of. But I didn't say anything. Her betrayal made me dizzy, and I recognized a dull pain in my stomach whenever it was on my mind. But I knew, or needed to believe about her, that she would not sleep with someone for what he could give her. And I didn't say anything because the only way that line of discussion could go was her telling me she loved him, had been in love with him...was still in love with him.

And that, I knew, I could not withstand. Maybe another day I could, when I was more sure of her in that moment, but not today, when I had a sense from her, and a fear, that she was marshaling everything in herself to stay in this room with me and not run out of the house to try to find him and set things right.

"I'm sorry," I said, dropping my hand to her shoulder. She leaned into it, turning her face to rest her cheek on my abdomen.

"You don't have to say you're sorry to me," she said. "Thank you, but you don't have to. I know what you're saying." She paused and took a deep breath. "I didn't do this horrible thing for anything I could get from him."

I waited to see if she would say why she did "this horrible thing," but she didn't. I suspected why, and I didn't want her to say those words. If she said them, I would have to do something about it.

"I want to tell Petra, make sure she knows," I murmured about Robert's wife, whom we had seen at university events since Catherine had started working there. They'd been to our house several times as well, I recalled with fresh discomfort and embarrassment. My skin was crawling with the thought of him sitting in our living room as if he owned it, and I rolled my shoulders to shake the feeling, remembering Robert nursing his beer at the parties we'd had, Catherine waiting on him. Petra standing by, sipping a glass of white wine, silent, observing and also somehow strangely proprietary, as if this room were now her family's just because for a little while they stood in it.

Catherine was standing in front of me. Her face looked wild with dread and anxiety, as her eyes searched my face. Her hair seemed to be standing up, making a kind of aura around her head with the lamp behind her diffusing light among the strands.

My thought was so loud I spoke it. "You look like a wild, frightened ghost." She turned her head, angling her chin, not changing her general impression, just adding to it a sense that she could not understand spoken words. She whispered, "Please, please do not talk to her. Think of her pain..."

"At least I respect her enough to tell her what really happened."

She took two deep breaths. I felt as if she were the therapist, I the patient. "If you're honest with yourself, you have to see that you don't want to tell her for her sake. You want to hurt him through her, and I think that's happened to her enough, don't you?" I started to answer, but she spoke over me as I drew breath, "Do you really think she'll thank you for that information? That she'll want to hear anything about her husband from *you*?" She emphasized the "you," an accusation.

She sat down again, wilting. I had no answer for her. I went to my desk, about three feet away, and sat, too.

"Did you hear what I said, about leaving the university?" she asked. "Do you want to know what I have in mind, have planned?"

We talked about it then, her ideas on what she could do here in Little Rock so that she wouldn't have to remain working there, for him, seeing him each day. I remembered the job she turned down at LSU, and waited for her to mention it, to suggest finding an academic position somewhere else, in another state, perhaps, but she didn't. Her management and research experience with "the private sector," as she kept referring to it, gave her several viable options, she insisted, and she had already sent several inquiries that afternoon to local contacts. But while she showed enthusiasm for new opportunities, she was simultaneously tense, and I wondered if it was because she was a little afraid of me, not just of what I might say, but what I might do, that could have repercussions beyond this room, this household. If I had wondered if there was a danger of her trying to rejuvenate her relationship with Robert or pursue him, I felt somewhat reassured by her determination to flee the scene of her crime. I knew she loved her job, but I wouldn't sympathize with her; I didn't want her to stay there, either, and I didn't want to diminish her drive to leave. If she remained and time passed, she would renew her attachment to the university and change her mind.

"It's shitty to leave during the semester," she said. I didn't answer her.

We had allowed six months for her to find something appropriate, before we would seriously discuss other options, but we knew that if she didn't get hired in a new position, we would probably move to find a job for her, either at another university or for a company. And the prospect of faculty positions would diminish with her abrupt departure from a tenure-line job. But within a month of beginning to look, she had an offer from a management consulting firm based in Chicago that wanted her to handle clients in Little Rock, Memphis, Dallas and other cities in the region, along with a local account team. She nearly doubled her salary, but both of us were relieved just to have the offer. I was reassured that something we had planned together had happened. She took the unprecedented and academic-career-killing action of quitting midsemester. She did not seem to be looking back.

About three weeks after she started her new job, I read in the paper that Robert had been hired to run a public-private venture capital fund in Little Rock, a somewhat high-profile role in Arkansas. When I had a break between patients that morning, I Googled the story and found a local business blog post reporting that Robert received a hefty signing bonus, among other perks. I felt a twinge of guilt that I hadn't stopped Catherine from leaving her job so quickly; with Robert gone, she could have stayed on at the university, working in her academic community, instead of the circus-freak oddity she felt herself to be in the consulting firm.

At the time, I thought this was the end of a terrible few months. I had no idea that I would wish longingly for these days, to have her back, to have her with me. Instead, a chapter of my life felt completed, and I was happy to turn the page.

• • •

There were several cars parked in the lot closest to my approach with the dogs, as there always were, and I felt a hard catch in my breathing as I saw that none of the cars was Catherine's. I knew the police had taken it for further search, but the last time I had been here, so had her car, and now I missed the comfort I had taken from that relic of her presence. Its absence was palpable.

I kept going toward the parking lot. I walked the dogs past the benches on the small terraced approach to the Big Dam Bridge, got all the way to the bridge itself, and then turned and walked toward the river, via the parking lot. There was a single, older bench there I sometimes sat on to rest before tackling the hill to return after a ride. The streetlights in the parking lot seemed to have some odd inability to permeate the grassy bank of the river above the lock, and I found myself half staggering toward the bench, unable to pace myself with the dogs. I could see only the glint of the bench's metal frame.

When I came around to sit down and let the dogs rest in the grass, though, I saw someone was already seated there, and I stepped back, automatically excusing myself.

"Hello, Lavinia," said a distant but familiar voice. Lavinia did not wag her tail, or approach him. In fact, she stiffened, alert.

"What are you doing here?" I stammered. Robert stood, and Lavinia growled, reminding me how intimidating a German shepherd, even a small one, could be. "What are you doing here?" and then, almost against my will, I sat down, leaving him to remain above me.

Lavinia moved between him and me. I could see in the dim light, the movement of his eyes, as he tracked her movements and mine. His multiple, dim shadows, cast by the parking lot lights near us and farther down, splayed out behind him, trickling out into the grass.

"I guess the same thing you're doing here," he said, and then drew in his breath in a short, sudden gasp. He stood there, hovering, saying nothing more.

I refused to give him a pass, though I didn't rise. "How fucking dare you! HOW FUCKING DARE YOU!" I yelled. Wesley came forward to stand by Lavinia but was silent. She continued a low growl, and I relaxed my hold on their leashes. I looked around for something to beat him with, something I could use to smash his polished, plastic face.

"I know. I know," he said, backing up, but every step he took, the dogs advanced, making up the ground, and more. "Hold your dogs, please." He looked at me, his face a white moon in the darkness, lit by the parking lot light right behind me. "I'm sorry. That was insensitive — and, well, just wrong, to just come up to you like that, and greet your dog like—"

"Like she's yours?" I felt like giving no quarter. "Just tell me what you're doing here. You don't have any kind of special privileges," I commanded, feeling powerful for the first time, I realized, since Catherine had confessed the affair to me. The dogs were my support. Lavinia's teeth were bright, even in the dark.

"I didn't plan to come this morning, but I wanted to, when I heard," he said, holding out his hand to Lavinia to calm her, as I was not doing so. She was silent, but lifted her upper lip more, exposing more white of her top fangs. He held his hand there. She did not blink.

"Lavinia, Wesley, sit," I commanded, taking a kibble out of my pocket for each of them. Wesley obeyed immediately, and Lavinia took her eyes off Robert for the first time since he had said her name, and swiveled her head around to me. I repeated my command, and she slowly dropped to a very shallow sitting position and returned her gaze to Robert, refusing the treat.

He dropped his hand and stood listing to one side on the uneven grassy slope, stuffing his ungloved hands into his trench coat pockets. "I have a flight at eight this morning. And when I was driving out of my neighborhood and realized I would be early, I just drove here. I've been wanting to come, but, of course, I didn't want to interfere or—"

"Implicate yourself?" I interrupted, studying his face.

"In?" He asked in response. "In her disappearance? No! No...You don't think that...? That I had something to do with it?" He tried to study me, but I knew my face was in darkness. It seemed to aggravate his frenzy. "Jesus! You didn't tell the police, did you?" He started toward me, and Lavinia sprang up out of her seated position toward him at the end of her leash. I held her back, but I didn't correct her.

"I haven't said anything yet," I said, "But if you two have emailed, texted or called since she got her new job, they'll know it before I do." I didn't like the threat as it emerged, because it exposed my fear that they were still involved in some way, and I hoped he wouldn't take the advantage.

"We have not been in any contact," he said. "Really. I promise you. I know you have no reason to believe me, but we haven't."

I pulled Lavinia back another couple of inches, and in response, she sat down next to Wesley, her gaze still fixed on Robert's form.

I had forgotten how tall he was, probably over six feet. "Catherine—" I stopped myself, feeling foolish for sharing with this man.

"What? What were you going to say?" he pressed.

"Catherine used to say she didn't trust tall men," I said. "That's all."

He looked, craning to see something in my face, but the darkness hid my expression.

"I just — I've been upset about her disappearance. I cared about her, no matter what you think my motives were." I felt the hairs on my neck rise.

"What do you think I think of you?" I asked, remembering how I had tried to disillusion Catherine that whatever she had felt for this man, he was very likely a serial cheater and she was probably a notch on his belt, maybe even literally.

"Are you head-shrinking me now?" he asked.

"Don't be an ass," I cautioned him. "I'm asking you how you might know what I would think if you hadn't been in touch with her after the split. I'm being the cuckolded husband, not the shrink, if you cannot tell the difference, you smug piece of shit."

"I'm sorry." We could hear the dogs breathing, the wash of the waves in the lock below, and then the feet of a runner coming down the bridge. I instinctively turned to watch him, and then turned back to Robert. The sky was beginning to turn pink over the horizon behind me.

"She told me you didn't like me before... the... before the end, that you would be particularly upset if you found out because you looked down on me enough to really be insulted."

"Even more insulted you mean," I said.

He gestured an imitation of acquiescence with an abbreviated wave of his hand, his head tilting in the same direction. "She didn't tell me anything after she told you about the affair — after she told me she was going to tell you," he said, correcting himself, "because we didn't talk after that, unless we were in meetings with other people. There was no relationship after there was no more relationship, if that makes sense."

Even though he was trying to convince me of his — and Catherine's — innocence, I could hear the sadness in his voice, and while I knew he was here on a morose errand, I thought he sounded more as if his sadness were about not having talked to Catherine for almost a year. And I believed him, not because I wanted to think well of Catherine, but because I could hear, and hate, his pain.

"I was sorry to hear about your son," I said, remembering the newspaper article about the accident. He looked down, bringing his hands out of his pocket and looking at them as he rubbed them together in the cold.

"Thank you. It's been...it's been terribly hard."

"I'm sure it was a shock." I heard my counseling voice.

"Yes..." he paused. "Now, I think...now you are head-shrinking me," he said, cautiously looking up at me. Wesley stood, wary, but Lavinia remained sitting, still looking at Robert, whose posture had changed with the topic of Tyler. He had wilted some, and I realized his stance with me had been combative, facing me directly, hands on hips or gesticulating into the air ahead of him, though he seemed so conscientiously amiable.

"I have nothing else to say except that," I confessed, coldly.

"I am sorry about Catherine. I pray for her quick return to you. I hope you'll allow me to say that much." He started to move toward the parking lot, but when Lavinia stood up, he stepped back, putting his right hand up in a casual, but, I thought, too-intimate wave.

"I have to get to my flight. I'm sure you'll never ask, but if there is anything I can do for you, I will do it." He was moving toward the two-door Mercedes that had gone by us up on Timberlake earlier. "I will do it," he said again.

"Robert—" I called as he was almost at his car. He turned.

"Yes?" He sounded hopeful...for expiation? Maybe not. Perhaps I just wanted him to feel supplicant to me, but I spoke and quashed the feeling.

"As I said, I haven't told the police anything about the...the two of you." He looked down again at his hands, this time holding his keys. He clicked his remote, and the lights blinked as the doors unlocked.

"That's what you said."

"As of now, I'm not going to, I mean—" I hated my awkwardness. "I mean, I have no plans to tell them, but if they find something, I won't deny it. I want to protect her. I do not want this in the *Democrat-Gazette* or the *Times.* But if there's something out there you know about, something you sent each other or called each other about, especially recently, then you should be ready."

He nodded.

"And you should at least fucking tell me before I read it in the paper."

"There's nothing," he said, quietly.

"Nothing? No random text? No chance meeting someone saw and suspected something? No email?"

"No. Honestly, no. To tell you the truth, I thought I would run into her somewhere, in a downtown restaurant at lunch, at the Capital Bar. Shit, on the running path." I blanched. I forgot that he was a runner, too. "But, I never did, never saw her. I didn't try to avoid her, to tell you the truth, so I suspect she was avoiding me. Maybe that's what the 5 a.m. running was about," he said, the vague sense of a question behind his statement.

I looked at him.

"She didn't used to run so early in the morning, if I remember. She went sometimes around UALR if the weather was good, or she ran at the fitness center, or on your treadmill, but she liked most to come here, to the River Trail, after work. I liked to come here then, too." He stopped, took a breath as if he were going to say something more, and then exhaled, a long slow breath.

He was right. The 5 a.m. running, either on our treadmill or at the river, had become her routine only after her confession to me last year. I hadn't even noticed.

"You run in the afternoon? Here?" I asked.

He answered, "I used to, when I was at UALR, but now, well, I still do when the opportunity comes, but it is not often."

• • •

After she changed jobs, we'd had a kind of "middle time," after the explosion and before the devastation. She quickly wrapped things up at the university. She'd had course releases, awarded to her probably through Robert, so her two-course load was transferred to other professors. In the meantime, she worked on building her consulting practice. She worked from an office in the Simmons Tower downtown that she shared with other consultants in the region when they were in Little Rock, and also with Chicago-based employees when they were on a team for a client project.

At first, I thought she would be working from home, like me, and that was a comfort to me, to have her where I could watch her. I wanted to trust her. I knew I needed to, but if I couldn't reach her on her cell or work number immediately, I had painful flashbacks to the months before, when every time I couldn't reach her gave me more cause to suspect the affair. Memories of those incidents made me go cold wondering where she was, what she was doing with him.

And she did work at home some, between big project pushes, or half days, she had the flexibility to do so, especially because the office was often a placeholder for the larger firm's fiction of a Little Rock fully-staffed location. Yet she seemed restless and uncomfortable because her workload was diminished as she built her client list. Within a month of being finished at UALR, she was getting up early, sometimes at 5 a.m. to go running or to work out in the house, and leaving between 7:30 and 8 in the mornings for her office, unless she was already out of town on a consultation to Dallas or a meeting in Chicago.

Catherine's doctor had recommended a therapist, so we began marriage counseling. I didn't want to see anyone in my old practice, or in my network. In our first session, the therapist told us not to rehash the details of the affair, that this was not the path to healing, that the focus must be on the two of us, what was not working, what had opened up rifts that another man could walk through. As the therapist spoke to us that first night, I was distracted by her lack of shadow. She sat right under a floor lamp that cast a warm, golden noon light down upon her soft, southern features.

"You're a therapist?" she said, looking to me with the open, value-neutral expression I, too, had cultivated throughout my career, yet somehow she seemed truly open, curious. "What kind of counseling do you focus on? Family? Marriage?"

"Rather general," I said, looking away from her. "But mostly family, including marriage, juvenile, some addiction and eating disorders, things that impact and derive from family settings."

"Yes, yes, well, that's what I do, too." She looked at Catherine. "What's that like, to be married to the Answer Man?"

I sat up straighter on the coral colored sofa that was too deep to relax into, but too shallow to use the throw pillows as cushions. Neither of them was looking at me. I knew that women didn't automatically bond, just by the virtue of being women, but I felt Dr. Robeson was consciously making an effort to ensure Catherine didn't feel overwhelmed by a counseling coalition.

"It's..." Catherine's eyes sidelined me, so I slid back to sag awkwardly against the couch, out of her peripheral vision. "He doesn't try to analyze me," she said, switching tacks. "But sometimes I feel like he does tell me what to feel. I...I mean, I don't think he does that as a therapist — don't therapists, aren't they against that, you know, mandating feelings?"

"Do you think he mandates your feelings, Catherine?"

"I think he does it as an older person, I mean, not elderly, not *old*, but just older than me. So, sometimes he just gives me advice, you know, like 'Don't think that,' or 'You don't need to feel that way.' I don't always want to have him solve things; I just want to tell him things, you know?" Catherine was speaking in slow, hesitant bursts, choosing words, preparing to say them, and then backing off them and choosing others.

"Occupational hazard," said Dr. Robeson.

"Well," I muttered. They both turned to look at me. "I wouldn't tell her what to think as a therapist, so it's not 'occupational,' is it? I'm just trying to help her out of her head. If she doesn't like it, I won't do it."

"Catherine," said Dr. Robeson, tacitly acknowledging my offer by asking my wife for her approval.

"It's not even a big deal," she said. "You just asked. He's usually right..."

"I want to know what to do right now," I interrupted. "It's murder around our house. I know what I would tell another couple, but that's not my role right now, right? I don't want to be the know-it-all. What did you say, the 'Answer Man'?"

Dr. Robeson tried to meet my gaze, but I looked beyond her at the small pastoral scene hung on the wall over her head. Her lamp transformed the shape of my head to a large misshapen orb on the wall.

"What specifically are you struggling with?" she asked, as if she were reciting by rote.

"I want to know what happened," I said. "I want to understand how this guy could get her attention, and, I can't help it, I want to know what happened between them, what their relationship was like."

"I don't know what that means," Catherine responded, without direction. "What was it like? Is there counseling lingo to categorize it? Am I supposed to talk about what we said to each other—"

"Not what you said." I stared at Dr. Robeson as a proxy for my wife.

But the psychologist took me up on it and didn't let Catherine answer.

"Although you feel as if you want to know all about the details, as the husband—"

"I feel like," I paused, and they both looked at me, though I noticed Catherine's quizzical gaze was tempered by a distant and fading posture. "I feel like my imagination is so vivid, so awful. It would be better to know from her what actually happened, so I could get a break from that."

"I know you feel that way, and it's completely understandable," said Dr. Robeson, looking at Catherine. "But the truth is you are where you are because of troubles in your own marriage, and that's what we're here to talk about. You know very well," she looked at me now, "that you can choose what to think about, what to focus on, what to prioritize, what to let go. You should really try to let that go as soon as you can. When you start to get pulled into those internal questions, ask yourself what provoked them. Is there something you need to talk to your wife about? Are you feeling lonely? Disconnected? Those answers are going to help you much more than the others because they keep you in your marriage and build intimacy. They keep you focused on making the marriage you want to happen."

• • •

After he drove away, I could not still my mind. Lavinia, aware I was anxious, kept circling me on her leash as I stood there, approaching me and nosing my arm. I petted her absently. I knew I had to walk back up the hill to my neighborhood, and my feet felt heavy, my bones and muscles enervated, as though I had a cold coming on. I turned to Wesley, who had lain down in the grass when Robert departed, and said aloud to him, "I had him here. I could have asked him anything, cursed him, told him anything, and I fucking told him I was sorry about his drunken son dying and—" I knew there was more, more to chastise myself for. Wesley watched me. "And then I made him my partner in more lies."

I walked over to the bench and sat down. I was overwhelmed by the information that Catherine's change to running in the early mornings was an effort to avoid Robert, an effort she made that he didn't, one that he observed, and I missed. Did she know he kept to his old routines when he could? Did she care? I hadn't asked him who had split with whom, and I still didn't know. The therapist hadn't allowed any discussion of specifics of her relationship with Robert in favor of us focusing on ourselves, and I complied to save face professionally. But the questions bit at my peace of mind.

This change in her routine was a small indication that she had left him, that it was she who had ended things. And the idea that her demonstration of willpower in favor of our marriage had gotten her abducted, or killed, broke my heart at the same time it bolstered my hope for us, for our future, a future I was starting to fear would never be. That I could have had it, a working, loving marriage, even for just a few months in the past year, if I had really forgiven her, really talked with her, was not a thought I could bear. It is still nearly too much for me, but I have had practice, and I have gotten used to feeling bad, as Chuck had promised I would.

I remembered we had some Xanax samples in the medicine cabinet at home. The scotch wasn't doing enough to numb me. I hadn't heard from Sandra yet, but when I did, I would ask her for something to help me sleep, to help mute the fear and rage that tinged my thought.

• • •

And so I tried to get around the therapist's bans with Catherine at home. Again, bullying her. I couldn't resist the satisfaction of the feeling that I was controlling her, moving her like a doll around the emotional playhouse of our marriage. I asked her when it had started, when they had kissed, fallen in love, slept together.

"Dr. Robeson says not to talk about it," she answered.

"You've never been one to be told what to do, so that answer seems a little facile to me."

"Facile? Have you been thinking of me as facile and waiting to call me that?" She didn't seem hurt or angry, just curious. I wouldn't let her be amused.

I took several steps toward her and yelled in her face, "Do you know how tortuous my imagination is on this subject?" She was shocked at the change in the weather of our discussion, but she didn't blanch or shrink from me. Tears sprang up in her eyes, I noticed with satisfaction.

"Then don't imagine it," she murmured. Her voice chilled and then iced over, her resignation was growing from day to day. "You can make up your mind to focus on the two of us instead of obsessing over anything that might have happened."

I tried to interrupt her, but she kept talking, looking me in the face. "If you ask me about it, I have to answer you, and I honestly don't want to talk about it with you or with anyone else. I want us to move on. I want us to focus on what could have caused this for us — not that it's not my fault or my responsibility, but I was reacting to something, or some things, and I want to figure that out. That's a solution. Talking over the problem is not the solution."

And she never told me. She never told me where they slept together, how they got away during the day, who made the first move, how their flirtation escalated, how many times they were together, who else went on the work trips they took while she was with him, or even how long the affair lasted. Of course, I tried to date the beginning of it, thinking back over the past several years, but I couldn't be sure. It could have been as long as 15 months ago, or maybe just five or six months. But he had been orbiting her since she started there.

The new construction of our old lives emerged from that dust and detritus that no one could see, not the people at the gala who chatted and laughed with us the first night I knew about it all, not Chuck, who had spent a lot of time with me alone and with us together, not our neighbors, not her colleagues or mine. We just put one foot in front of the other, and if she missed him or thought of him or wanted him, I didn't know. I refused to ask.

In what turned out to be our last therapy session, our marriage counselor tried to focus us on forgiveness. Immediately, I asked what she had to forgive me for. I knew I was petulant. I looked at Catherine, but she was inscrutable, merely watching the doctor for more information in order to comply, to understand. Catherine had always been a very good student. I realized what she was doing when she wouldn't answer my questions about their relationship; she was being a good student of our therapist instead of being a good student of mine, which I had been used to before she transferred that authority to Robert. She was probably being a "good student" when she fucked her boss, the quasi-academic, too, I thought.

"Did you have some kind of daily routine?" I asked her one morning as she put her coffee cup in the dishwasher, and then pulled it out again refilling it and sitting back down at the table with her paper. She seemed unsure of what to do with herself, to linger over her coffee or to get ready and go to the office.

"What? Where, at UALR?"

"With him?"

"We're not supposed to—"

"GODDAMN IT! You weren't supposed to have sex with anyone else, either, were you? Why not break a rule for me? Just do it for me, because *I want you to...*" I stressed the last words. She didn't look up. She had begun to get red in the face, as she did when she seemed embarrassed for me.

And that was a question she answered. She wouldn't tell me anything about the sex they had, her love for him, how or where he kissed her, but she answered that question.

"Sometimes he called me on his way to work in the morning. He knew my class schedule, so he knew where I'd be each day. We'd talk about our schedules that day and figure out if we could see each other."

"You weren't together every day?" I was disbelieving, sure she was lying to pad her defense.

"No. Most days, no," she said. She was facing the window, with her eyes up and to the right, as she did when she was recalling something with care and precision. "We were both busy, with many calls on our time, and transparent lives, you know, the academic busy-bodies, and his family really knew him very well and they knew he was behaving in a different way, so not every day, no. Once or twice a week."

I didn't ask what happened on those days, once or twice a week.

• • •

Somehow, I walked the dogs home, up the long hill and through the neighborhood, the subtleties of the colors of Little Rock winter starting to broaden in the browns of the bare trees and the silvers of the roads and sky. I was thinking of the scotch and the Xanax. The sun was well up by the time I put the key in the back lock, and I imagined Robert boarding his plane to somewhere, taking his first-class seat, sipping his own scotch at 9 a.m. I wondered if he was as unsettled from the post-adrenaline burst of the encounter as I was.

I took the small sample box of Xanax out of the medicine cabinet in our tiny, outdated master bathroom, and saw there were only two pills left. I didn't remember where we'd gotten this, but I hadn't been taking them. Six were gone. I took one with water from the tap cupped in my hand. I thought about breakfast, but my stomach was still upset from the drinking and lack of sleep the night before. I made some coffee and opened the liquor cabinet to find some brandy.

There was a longer story in the paper that morning, and I could see the direction the reporter was beginning to take: Successful, middle-class, white woman (blonde even) goes missing from the jewel of Little Rock's recreational crown — the Big Dam Bridge is the longest pedestrian-only bridge in the United States. The reporter quoted runners, walkers and cyclists who frequented the path who either said they felt safe, or did not feel safe and when and why. One woman spoke in detail of a detour she had taken after seeing a man inappropriately dressed for walking or running sitting on a North Little Rock bench near the trail, cellphone in hand: "I didn't know, but something wasn't right, and I wondered if he was signaling someone ahead that I was coming. Then I saw someone walking up the bank from the river, so, I just lit out of there," she said. There would be a lot more anecdotes now that were similar, I thought, people joining in the fear and urgency. People flock to belong to anything, even crushing pain.

That was a sidebar story. The main news piece, which started on the bottom of the front page, was about the investigation of the "missing runner."

I was exhausted and skittish about what I might find, so I didn't focus or read carefully then, but I scanned it for any hint or intimation of where the investigation might be going now that they had turned from me. I hadn't heard from the police since noon the day before. They had now identified her publicly, and there was a small mug shot, which was her professional portrait from the consulting firm. I felt a moment of gratitude that at least the paper hadn't used her UALR photo; did it mean they weren't looking at her life there? And then? This photo was bland, what she called her consultant's "navy suit photo."

An officer was quoted as saying the LRPD had indications Catherine had been followed to the river. This was new to me; none of the officers had said anything like this in our brief conversations. I thought about calling Brooke, but kept reading, and came to this paragraph:

> Det. Schmidt, of the LRPD Violent Crimes Division, who works with missing-persons cases, said that while cameras are positioned and operating as programmed at the Big Dam Bridge parking lot, the data from the digital recorders revealed nothing more than a dark-colored, late-model sedan circling the recreational parking area within minutes of Zrzavy parking, preparing for and starting her run, which appeared to be toward the east, in the direction of Riverdale, along a path that parallels Rebsamen Road.

Detectives are interested in the sedan and are examining security footage as well as other sources to identify it and locate the driver for any information he or she may have as witnesses to when Zrzavy was last seen.

I had been told none of this, and I struck Robert from the list of suspects, though I honestly hadn't thought of him as one until he surprised me at the river this morning — and not really even then. I thought again of the journals hidden in my neighbor's house and began to believe I would need to read through them. I briefly stiffened against the thought, and then slowly relaxed. Until this time, I had assumed that Catherine's abduction, which it certainly must have been as neither she nor her body had been found, was a random crime, perpetrated by someone with opportunity without specific intention. Because if it wasn't Robert, who would follow her to the Bridge parking lot at 5 in the morning? I thought again of calling Brooke, but I decided to let her call me if there were any need. Or let Chuck call me; they seemed to operate as one when it came to my case.

I walked restlessly around the house for 30 or 40 minutes, thinking of the journals, afraid to get them out in case doing so revealed to someone that they were there. I had a visceral resistance to the idea of reading her thoughts in the morning newspaper along with the rest of the state. I had just as strong of an aversion to reading them myself, and imagining Robert's slick photo in the articles about her disappearance was anathema to me. I went and sat down on the deck while the dogs were investigating the yard, thinking the cold would brace me.

The car following Catherine seemed to be leading the police away from me, and it was this assumption that emboldened me, and I decided that when evening came, I would go in the dark to where the journals were hidden and remove the most recently written one or two. If Catherine had a capacity for secrecy that would allow her to cheat, she may have been hiding other things from me, things that might now help me understand why someone would target a management consultant from Little Rock for an abduction, and hopefully a ransom, but not — no, not — a murder.

I must have dozed off, finally, because, after reading the article, I looked up and saw Catherine sitting on the deck with me, wearing her running clothes, her earbuds in her ears. The dogs had no reaction. They stared out into the yard as if she weren't there. But when there was a sudden, faint waft of Shalimar on the wind, Lavinia's head turned, and her nose twitched into the breeze.

I was afraid to move, afraid to breathe, afraid the slightest movement would cause her to disappear. She was sitting parallel to me, also looking out at the woods down the hill. Contemplative, pensive, a slightly sad expression, yet peaceful. The resignation she had come to wear so easily emanated from her. How had I not seen it before?

I couldn't keep myself from trying to make some contact.

"Catherine?" I noticed that though her eyes moved, following a bird in the trees, that her foot tapped — to music? — that she moved her arm to rest it on the Adirondack chair arm, her chest did not rise and fall with breath. Her skin was pale, white even.

She turned her head slowly in my direction, but seemed to look through me.

"Catherine?" I said, with more conviction. Lavinia looked at me.

Catherine mouthed something and pointed to her ears.

"What? What is it? Catherine? Where are you?"

She moved her mouth again, and no sound emerged.

I saw what she was trying to say: "I cannot hear you."

• • •

"We all have ways in which we let others down," Dr. Robeson said, rather pointedly to me. "But this is not what we are focusing on here today, and you're right when you say that she has done the wrong, and yet you are being called upon to make it right by choosing to forgive her."

I sat, stubborn, watching Catherine, who allowed a brief shadow of sadness to flicker when the therapist said the words "she has done the wrong."

"Why, as you asked last week, should you have to do all the work when she is the cheater? Is that what you said? Am I correct in my memory?" As a therapist, I knew when I was being led toward something. Catherine's face again reflected this light shade of grief, and my stubbornness melted somewhat. I knew this woman was honestly trying to help us get somewhere good, somewhere we both told her we wanted to go.

"That's what I said, yes, almost word for word," I answered at last.

"And why should you change how you are when she is in the wrong?"

I nodded.

"And you know, as a professional therapist, I imagine, what my answer will be to that?"

I nodded again.

"Do you want me to say it, or would you like to do so?"

"Because neither she nor I can change the past, and you are attempting to equip me with a sense of power over what happens to me in this relationship and in this marriage by giving me something to do, something to work on, so that I am not just a leaf in this awful wind."

She nodded again.

She turned to Catherine. "You look sad. How are you feeling right now?"

"I feel...I feel," she looked down at her hands, and I saw tears on her cheeks, nose and lips. She had cried in these last few minutes and her whole face was damp. I hadn't heard her. "I feel so awful about how much pain I caused him." She turned to me on the couch beside her and squeezed my hand, and I returned the gesture, which seemed to soothe her somewhat so I stopped, because I wanted to hear this pain out, I wanted it to assuage me. I wanted to take what I suspected might be one of the last opportunities to wear this cloak of martyrdom with her.

"I know how the affair happened," she said. "I know why, but that is not an excuse. I knew it was wrong when I was doing it, and I knew I was keeping it a secret from the person with whom I had always been so comforted not to have secrets from, and I knew the distance was growing, and that I was healing it with someone else, and I knew, I knew, I knew."

She looked so foreign in her brown "company man" suit, like an automaton, programmed, so different from the red-inside-her Catherine I had met at Chuck's. There was a long, gray shadow across her face because she was sitting with her back to the lamp. I couldn't see the fractious nuances of her expression.

"I didn't rationalize," she went on. "I chose to do wrong, because I felt so loved with this other person, and though my husband said he loved me, I did not feel loved around him as I did with...this other man." She withdrew her hand, and I felt alarmed. I stared down at my lap thinking this was the moment she was going to leave me. *She was going to leave me.* This had to be the pinnacle of her selfishness.

But she interrupted my internal raging. "I was so wrong, because he has done so many things," she looked at me to make it clear she was talking about me, her husband, "to give me the life I have. I don't just mean materially. I mean in so many ways — encouraging me in things that I feared, like pursuing my Ph.D., when it was in a field he didn't really respect before, and how he came to respect it because he listened to me as I explored it and worked on my dissertation. I mean, that one thing is so indicative of how much he loves me: He changed his opinion about something because I thought of it differently than he did, and he took my experience as his own so much that he changed his mind.

"I was young when we met, young myself, *and* younger than he was, and so, maybe, I've changed more," she continued. "I have always been a runner, though, and he didn't really do anything, and he tried running with me just to be with me, but he hated it, so he started cycling. That was also so amazing to me, that I could influence this man who had so much figured out." She paused. "Just, just things like that," she whispered. "I should have told him that I noticed. I never told him." She looked down, and spoke, then, with her eyes closed.

"And this is what I did? This is how I returned that love? When there was a problem, I just gave my love to someone else. But it wasn't mine to give to someone else, really, was it?" She asked the therapist, not me. "I had already given it to my husband. It was false to try to give that love to someone else."

"Is that why you started acting like I was such an asshole?" I asked her. Dr. Robeson turned to moderate my outburst, but Catherine, anticipating this, quieted her. "It's all right," she said. "I've been thinking about that," she answered me. "Because you've mentioned that before, and when you first asked me, I didn't know the answer."

Dr. Robeson asked me what it was I'd said. "I asked her why, when she knew she was being dishonest with me and cheating on me with this clown, why she didn't feel guilty enough to at least be nicer to me when we were together."

"Yes, and I think I know why now." She looked at Dr. Robeson for permission to answer this question, which she was mutely given. "Of course, I had the selfishness of the cheater. I mean, I couldn't have had an affair if I hadn't somehow given myself permission to do what I wanted and get what I needed, even if the doing and the getting were wrong. So part of it was just being childish, and self-interested and just going with it, indulging it." She gathered herself a little in a way I had learned to recognize meant she was about to say something she believed would hurt me, a quick inhalation, closing her eyes for just a fraction of a second longer than a blink, making little, momentary fists.

"A deeper part of it was that I just missed Robert when I wasn't around him, and I was crankier and less charitable because I wasn't where I wanted to be. I was where I should be." I started to answer her, to say sarcastically that I was so sorry to have come between her and her lover. She kept talking though.

"But," she said very quietly, looking at Dr. Robeson, not me, "I think the reason I wouldn't let myself realize that then, or even a few weeks ago when you first asked me that question, is that I really was angry and disappointed with you, with how things were going for us, and I never would let myself act on that before. I wouldn't confront you or tell you things weren't what I wanted them to be. I didn't talk about it with you because I didn't even think about it. I didn't know there was a problem. Shit, I told Robert that I loved you and was very happy with you, and I fucking meant it!"

Her face was red, she was crying more tears now, and she had that wild, desperate look, but I would have known she was intensely rattled even if I couldn't see her, because she never used language like that with anyone but me and her closest friends.

"But obviously, there were things wrong — things we've talked about here — that I understand better now, and I was angry about them, and without the cloak of this affair or my childishness over not having everything that I wanted, every second that I wanted it, I finally let myself feel the frustration and disappointment that was there for me, with us, with you, with our life." She was quiet, still. After a couple of slow, deep breaths, she finished. "That's the answer. That is why."

Dr. Robeson looked at me, and I couldn't find any words for a response because I believed her, and I wondered why I hadn't seen the answer for myself, why I had even asked the question.

We briefly revisited some of the issues we'd identified: my paternalism, which the therapist sympathized with, again, as an "occupational hazard" of those in my profession, particularly men; my argumentative and sarcastic nature and its corroding effect on a marriage when Catherine was so prone to acquiescence to gain approval from someone older, someone in authority; her depressive periods, and how during these times she relied on me to do the things she disliked so much in me when she wasn't depressed.

"It's such a cliché."

"What is, Catherine?" asked Dr. Robeson, but I knew. Catherine looked at me to answer and nodded for me to go ahead.

"That what attracts us most is what tears the relationship apart and damages it the most." Catherine nodded again.

"Next time, we'll talk this over in more depth if you like," Dr. Robeson said, again looking at me, and moving her eyes without hiding it to the clock.

"Before we go," I said, "I know about the role forgiveness plays in the marriage, or the future of the marriage..."

"Try to be less professional, less impersonal," the counselor admonished me. I corrected myself in order to make my point; we had such limited time now. Minutes maybe.

"I know I need to forgive Catherine if our marriage is really going to thrive," I said, and Dr. Robeson nodded. "I want to do that. I don't know how to do that unless I feel she is as sorry as I feel she should be. I know that's not what I should be doing, feeling—" I cut off Dr. Robeson as she moved forward in her chair to question me. "But that's how I feel. I mean, if she's not sorry enough, how can I trust her? And if I can't trust her, how can I forgive her?"

Keeping her eyes on me, Dr. Robeson spoke, sitting on the edge of her seat, the lamp light hitting her so square it looked like daylight on her face, her feet pointed forward to me directly, her hands firmly on the arms of her chair, ready to rise, but not rising. "Your questions are not unusual, as you know. I want you to listen to my answer and think it over before next time.

"Forgiveness is a choice you make. It is not contingent on what she does; it can't be, because then it's a natural consequence, not an act of your own will. Catherine's infidelity has wronged you, and in doing so, she has put herself in your debt. She owes you. You feel this, of course you do, it is such a simple truth: *She owes you.*" I nodded. I did not look at Catherine. I could hear her breathing.

"Your forgiving her is your choice, and it is your way of saying to her, 'You owe me, and I am wiping away your debt. You no longer owe me. There is nothing in that ledger. I have wiped it clean with an act of my will.'"

I blinked. I had worked with unfaithful couples before, successfully, and I had never explained forgiveness in this way, perhaps I hadn't said such a thing because I would have found it so difficult to believe as a man, so unfathomable that a wronged man could make such a choice as I was being asked to make.

"Trust is another issue," she said, standing, "And we will address that in the future. Now, our time is up. Are you set up for another appointment?"

Catherine explained that our schedules were up in the air while she tried to settle a work trip to California that I might be joining her for, so she would make another appointment when we returned, once that was settled.

"Well, I've given you plenty to think about for the road," Dr. Robeson smiled, kindly, without softening the challenge her words contained for me. "I'll see you when you return."

But we hadn't gone back. Our trip had gone well, we were busy, Catherine's schedule was harried and hectic with her growing client load, and by the fall, I realized we probably wouldn't return to Dr. Robeson. I also knew this wasn't accidental, and we hadn't returned because neither of us wanted to. I didn't know Catherine's reasons, aside from her work demands, and I didn't ask her, but I remembered the shadow that had crossed her face when the therapist referenced the wrongs she had done our marriage, and me.

In order to assuage myself, I made up my mind.

"I trust you," I said to her one morning, as she was about to leave for work. We'd been silent in the kitchen with the dogs and the morning routines. The leaves were turning all around the house by now, and the sunlight through them seemed to light the kitchen on fire. She froze, her hand on the back door knob. "I mean, I'm choosing to trust you."

"What's bringing this out, just now?" She asked. She didn't turn to me.

"I know you saw what all this has done not just to me, but to us. My pain has been painful for you, too. I think you were naïve — innocent, *innocent* in a way about what an affair would do, would be like, would lead to. I think you've been changed, and even if you haven't, I'm throwing in with you. I'm going to trust you." I was saying all of this to her back, the line of her shoulders through her suit jacket remained steady, unchanged, as I spoke.

That night over dinner, I brought it up again, perhaps to convince myself. "I think we both learned some things we didn't know about each other, about the relationship," I reassured her at Casa Manana on Cantrell, where the dark interior made me feel more like confiding in her than our sunlit kitchen or sitting room, or at least the proximity meant she couldn't turn her back to me. "If something starts to feel wrong again, one or both of us will recognize it in a way we didn't — couldn't — before." I held her hand across the table, and felt her physical relief as I spoke.

I hadn't told her I had forgiven her, but I hoped from the way I treated her, praised her, comforted her, that she felt forgiven. And maybe it would be true someday. Someday, I would make up my mind to erase her debt to me.

• • •

When the sun set, bolstered by four cups of black coffee and a shot or two of scotch, I went out the back gate of our yard and followed the path over to Mrs. Judson's to retrieve the Kroger bag of journals and brought it into the house, into my office through the backyard client entrance. Somehow, I felt that if I had these private things in here, in this inner sanctum of so many wounded psyches, where people were safe with what they said to me, the thoughts in these journals would be safe from the world, as well. And perhaps I felt that I would be able to approach what was in them bolstered by a therapist's distance rather than a husband's desires and disappointments.

I had never touched these books before. Catherine had written in them sporadically since I had met her, and once we lived together, she kept them up without writing every day, sometimes changing the time of day she wrote for awhile, part of a new routine, sometimes with coffee in the morning, sometimes after dinner, sometimes in bed. But while she wrote her entries in front of me, I never saw the books themselves lying around, and in fact, hadn't known until recently that she kept them in shoe boxes in the closet. I'd felt guilty when I accidently found them while looking for a pair of boots of hers I wanted to replace for her as a gift.

In the front covers of all the journals, Catherine had written the date of when she started it, and when she came to the end, she recorded that date in the front, as well. I sorted through all of them — there were 12 — and put them in order, from her high school years until last week. The most recent journal was about half-filled and active, and the previous journal, which I saw from a quick scan of the dates, was written leading up to, during and immediately after the affair and had two full signatures of empty pages at the end, abandoned. She had started the current one not long after she confessed to me.

I picked up what I came later to think of as "the affair journal" and held it in my hands, simultaneously curious and averse to it. It was, like most of the recent editions of this chronicle of her life, a Moleskin book, bound in soft, dark-brown leather. The most recent journal was black, of the same make and size. I held the brown book in my hands, but though I felt some need to hurry, to get them back to their new hiding place before anyone saw me with them, I couldn't open it right away. I probably held it for several minutes, with little starts of adrenaline welling up as I tried to will myself to open it. I couldn't help feeling what a violation this was of my wife, her inner life, her trust in me, her agreement to share my life, my world, my space with that fundamental expectation that she could decide what of her life she would share with me.

I had never asked her if I could read what she wrote in these books; sometimes she would read a section aloud to me if she were trying to tell me how she felt about something that moved her or upset her, but I never asked to sit down with the books and take in all that was there, turning page after ecru page, with her little weather notations, running mileage goals, notes about what she wore, errands to do, etc. I wouldn't have asked. I think she wouldn't have said yes. This kept me sitting there, unmoving, for some time. I could hear the faint electric whir of the clock I kept in view to monitor my patients' session times.

I did not know what to do, and again, I felt the bifurcation of my mind, part of my conscious mind telling me I could wait, I didn't need to read them today, the other part aware that I would sit here until I read them.

I would cope with what she thought of that when she got home.

There might be information in either one of these journals that could help us find her now, and though it seemed logical to start with the more recent journal, there was something pressing me to open and read the earlier one, the journal that covered the time of the affair. I suspected it was largely some part of my psyche that wanted to take advantage of this opportunity to read it with an "excuse" or rationale. But the pull to that journal was also based on the knowledge I'd had for more than a year, that Catherine could keep secrets from me, and that maybe some of those secrets had to do with what had happened to her now.

I quickly leafed through the book I most feared, but held it at a distance. She wrote on one page, "I'm told not to write of all this, but it is my small rebellion, my secret." That was all that was on the page. I imagined Robert telling her not to leave any traces of what was happening between them, and her coming home, taking out the small Moleskin book she kept in her scarf drawer and writing just that sentence, and then putting it away for months, disobeying and obeying simultaneously. So she kept secrets in her clandestine life, as well.

I started to turn the page, but instead I shut it and picked up the most recent journal and opened it. I didn't want to intrude so deeply into her dark places, nor did I want to be completely awash in all the details, whatever she did write, of the affair again. Not now, when just living into the next second was so overwhelming most of the time, I couldn't face it, couldn't make the most minute of plans.

Thumbing through, I could see that she had begun this journal in March of last year, about two months after her confession. Scanning the pages of her small, scratchy handwriting as I flipped through the book, I decided to start at the most recently written entries and work back. If I found something the police needed to know, I could tell them she told me about it, and I had forgotten it. I was afraid to produce one journal, thinking they may come for more of them. If I didn't get to anything useful in this book, I would work my way back to the other journal, and I could read it once I was ready.

The last entry was three days before she disappeared.

January 11

    Chicago trip cancelled yesterday. Client worried about minor project, not committing on major effort. So backward. So...time at home after all. H a little loaded up with patients now. Not too much afternoon lollygagging in store, I guess. Weight down a little, surprising after Christmas binge-binge-binge. Still working on energy consultation, so that's a time suck, but enjoyable. Craving something. Massage? A great run? Two movies in a row? Travel? Strange unsettledness. Maybe just work letdown? Nostalgic, I guess, too.

I smiled seeing how she referred to me as "H" or "Husband" in her journals, too. If she emailed me or left me a note, wrote me a card, she always called me that. Seeing that she did it privately to herself made it even dearer to me. Most of her entries going back about a month or so, anywhere from one to five a week, were similar, though most were longer, some with more detail. She made notes on work, sometimes on my schedule/work demands, lunch with a friend, a conflict with her boss that she was proud of herself for resolving. A thread of some vague dissatisfaction with no explicitly assigned cause or root. Sentences like that note, "Nostalgic, I guess, too," echoed through these several pages. And then there was this one:

October 16

　　Saw him two days ago. Reminds me of that Ted Kooser poem. Isn't that funny — I think I know about two poems, and that is one. And now I understand it so much better. Should be capital H: Him. But won't do that because of H. Him and Husband cannot be the same.

　　I don't know if he saw me at first, but it was something to me that I looked pretty, had lost a little weight (he likes thin women, fit people in general), so I felt like if he did see me, he would be pleased. (This is so lame. But I mean, if I'm going to see and be seen, why can't I "win"?) We were at the annual business school luncheon, and I guess he was there for his job. I went with Mena. She had a seat. She asked me to come, and I honestly didn't think of him going. I wouldn't have gone if I had thought. I wanted to see my colleagues from the SOB. Honestly, I miss them so much. I miss academia. I miss the autumn on campus. The evening light with the earlier setting sun always makes me miss the end of a long day at a university. Now, I drive home in that light, up Cantrell Hill out of downtown toward the Heights, and that light. That light. It kills me, because it means more on a college campus than it means to a fucking corporate management consultant trying to book after-work to plump up her billings. Jesus. I miss it.

　　So I saw him. And I think I saw him looking at me. And just to see him this time of year, when I am most missing the world I'm really made of, made for, was shit. And it laid me low. I am not sure I heard much of what Mena was saying. I hope I faked it well enough that she didn't know. I'm still worried people know/are talking/talked about us. He was sitting with his VC people. Big swinging dicks. The VIPs. Now he controls So. Much. Money.

And then I tried to gather myself, compose myself. FOCUS. FOCUS. Talk to my friends, chase the bit of chicken around the plate, eat salad, talk to my friends. And then he was there, standing over Mena's shoulder, looking right at me. I had that strange feeling of my skin being so alive I could feel every inch of my clothes, my blouse, my jacket, my bra. He was there. HE.

I don't know how to explain it to myself, but since I left the university and have been successfully avoiding him, it's as if he is some kind of celebrity. I see photos sometimes in the paper, or my friends from UALR talk about him, but he is abstract. Unreal. He doesn't move and breathe anymore. So it was as if someone so famous was suddenly standing before me; I lost my moorings a little. I think I actually clutched the table.

He was looking right at me while he talked to everyone at the table. He'd glance around as a kind of courtesy, a disguise more like, and then just bring his eyes back to me and hold my gaze. It was too much for me, like a rich meal. I kept looking down at my plate, my hands, but when I looked up again, he was still looking at me, and would hold my gaze again — still. It was thrilling. Really thrilling. This secrecy was electrifying to me. Everyone was talking...blah blah blah, venture capital, development, cloying, obsequious, a habit of his days at UALR and an iteration of his new power. I didn't like it. He's better than that, more than that, could be. I stood before I thought about it. I excused myself and walked out to the Ladies'. It's a long walk through that dining room. I thought I might throw up. Or cry. I was so emotional. I just walked.

And I thought about coming to similar functions with him when we were kind of noticing each other, and when we were sleeping together, and now here we were, two completely different people, sharing this awful, wrong, painful, hurtful, sexual secret over the heads of people who are meant to know us both well. It just was so strange and terrible and I wanted it and I didn't want it. So I just walked away.

I was a little teary in the bathroom. Just from emotion, I guess. I felt like I might throw up, too. I missed him, I felt guilty for what I did to H, what I ruined at home. What I lost from both Robert (friendship) and H (what didn't I lose? Trust, belief, admiration...on and on and on).

When I came out, he was standing there. I almost walked back in the Ladies' room but he looked nervous, somehow approachable in a way he didn't look in the banquet hall. There he looked smarmy. Posturing. Like he was trying to own that whole room — and me. Here he looked smaller, unsure. It melted me. I was afraid of being seen, but I went to him.

He told me how pretty I looked, which annoyed me, but satisfied me, too. He was wearing that navy pinstripe I like so much. But with a white shirt, which he never used to do. We chatted a little. He asked me about my job. Blah Blah Blah. I had this voice in my head yelling at me, "You have two minutes with him, maybe for the rest of your life. Don't talk about this!" But I couldn't think of anything else to say. Couldn't change the subject. Then I remembered. I told him I was so very sorry about Tyler. I thought he was going to start crying right there, which was shocking, and I was glad I had said it, gotten some real emotion from him, and then I felt cruel for that, but I missed the realness of being with him when he wasn't Big Man On Campus all the time. He was quiet. I started to say something, and then he spoke, and it was so odd.

I'm trying to remember EXACTLY what he said. It was so strange. He said he was sorry, but that I should be careful. I asked what about? In what way? He said he couldn't talk about it here/now, but Tyler was mixed up in something, and it was "spilling over" to other things, to him. I asked him what he meant. He shook his head. A woman I didn't know walked between us to the restroom. We backed up toward the wall in the corner of the landing. I asked again. I asked him if he was okay, safe. He said he had lost his son, so he would not likely be okay again. He didn't care about it, about being safe, but he cared about me being okay and safe. I said straight out, "What are you saying to me? Are you saying I'm involved in something?" Was he accusing me? Of what? Because he was looking at me with some fright and concern. I wouldn't have asked that, but for the expression on his face. He saw someone he knew on the landing below, and he said again, "Just be really careful. Okay? I do, I care so much about you. I really do—" and he walked away.

I think this is so shitty of him to do, to drop this vague bomb on me and stroll on out to his big world. I don't know what the hell he is talking about. Tyler is dead. How can whatever he was involved with concern me? I didn't really even know him. I don't know what he was involved with aside from drinking too much and getting fired from or quitting all his jobs. How can I be careful if I don't know what the danger is? And he loves me, or he "cares about" me. He said "cares." But I heard that he loves me. Is that just what I want to hear? Or did I feel it so strongly, I heard it instead of what he said? And did he say "cares," because he doesn't dare say "love" aloud? I'm glad I didn't have a chance to/wasn't expected to respond. I could never say those words aloud to another man and not think of the pain I would be causing H. I could not do it, but I would have wanted to protect Robert, too, not leave him exposed. What would I have said? I don't know. Glad I didn't have to answer. Not sure about love/in love...

I think I have picked up the phone to call him 10, 20 times in the past two days. But I don't want to do it. I can't justify talking to him at the banquet, but I cannot rationalize at all taking action to talk more to him, and then I think it's all some dramatic ploy to get me to chase after him again, because of how we split, and how he wants it all, to be the good and dutiful husband and civic lion, and to be wanted and adored (chased?) by me. And I feel angry.

And, honestly, I feel a little scared. Because he looked scared and worried for me. And he looked like he was to blame.

I willed my mind to quiet, but the caffeine was surging through the miasma of my thoughts, physically unsettling me. I looked up the poem she was thinking of. I stood and went to the bookshelf in our bedroom, plucking the thin volume from the shelf and then returning to my office, avoiding everything else I had just read. We had a signed book by Kooser from an event we had attended, a reading by the Poet Laureate at Hendrix College. I paged through the book and stopped on this:

> After Years
> Today, from a distance, I saw you
> walking away, and without a sound
> the glittering face of a glacier
> slid into the sea. An ancient oak
> fell in the Cumberlands, holding only
> a handful of leaves, and an old woman
> scattering corn to her chickens looked up
> for an instant. At the other side
> of the galaxy, a star thirty-five times
> the size of our own sun exploded
> and vanished, leaving a small green spot
> on the astronomer's retina
> as he stood in the great open dome
> of my heart with no one to tell.

I reread those lines over and over, moving my eyes over the type for more than a minute, "the great open dome / of my heart with no one to tell." No one to tell. She is right. She couldn't have told me, because I would have been so irate and humiliated simultaneously, I would not have cared about her "open dome heart." But standing back, back, back from all the explosions in this minefield of a journal entry, even I could see that as a husband looking for his wife, Robert had to be faced.

I scanned again the more recent entries I had already read, maybe for some detail I had seen but hadn't understood, connected to this conversation, this interaction, but there was nothing. It was as if all the other entries were from some other person's journal, except for the vague and clouded nostalgia, she mentions none of these things again, not Tyler, not Robert, not being scared or getting warned. I put the journal down, exhausted, brittle.

I put the dogs out, but my hands were shaking, and I felt similar to how I had felt after I had seen Robert at the bridge. *He had lied to me; he saw her, and he even tried to warn her.* I was devastated by the thought that this all could have been avoided if he had been clear with her, if she had talked to me.

I sat down to read a few more journal entries that preceded the October 16 writing, hoping they would calm me, but they were similar to more recent jottings, work, weather, vague unsettled feelings, more or less dissatisfaction.

October 4

    Strange little cold snap. Wore boots today and cashmere — short-sleeved, but still. Nice. Exhausted by heat these last days. All morning long crisis <u>du jour</u> with Chicago. Conference call after conference call. These people have to gangbang every little detail. They would lose their shit if they had to experience for 10 minutes the autonomy of academia. 18 emails later, back to where we had started, but now everyone *okay with it. WTF? Great use of all our time. Great way to bill client exorbitant $ for no real progress. Funny lunch. Ran down to Hanaroo for takeout happy chad roll. To reward myself for living through ridiculousness. Same two guys came in after me as came in after me last week. Just noticed because they are not office or politico types you find around these bank towers near the Capitol. My fortune didn't say if they would be there next week.* [Here she had drawn a smiley face.] *Casting about for things to notice, make meaningful. Stupid job. Understimulated by good things. Overstimulated by the bad. Home alone or home with someone who isn't home. The awful affair gave me something to notice, be thrilled and intrigued by. So not fair, but so understandable, if you ask me. But nobody does.*

A September 30 entry about the weather also mentioned complaints about work, but she also mentioned that she felt she was "supposed" to be happy, though didn't clarify that she wasn't. "Bad feelings going into summer, bad feelings coming out," she had written, then in capital letters, "DO LOVE H."

I kept paging back, not reading closely the entries that were like this one, even though I felt I should because wouldn't that be where I might find something really important, buried in the mundane? I felt naïve, thinking I could find the case-solving clue because of my intimate knowledge of my wife, knowledge no one else had, but as I read, that slipped away.

I walked back to Mrs. Judson's to return the other journals, and I thought of Catherine last fall. I didn't remember my wife in the ways she was describing herself in these pages. I returned to my office with the dogs trailing close behind. They'd been out for the last time for the night, and they expected treats before retiring to their dog beds.

I got out my appointment calendar, which Catherine liked to mock because it was on paper, not in the computer. Hers were all linked, synced, among work, home, iPhone, and I just had this old-fashioned spiral-bound book. I opened my filing cabinet where I kept all the old calendars. I bought the same one every year, and I had at least 15 years of a matched set — and took last year's off the top. I looked up my schedule for the days I had read of hers. On October 16, when Catherine wrote about her earlier meeting of Robert at the banquet, I had a full day of patients, from 8 a.m. to 8 p.m. It occurred to me she had written such a lengthy, contemplative entry upstairs, alone in one of her little reading areas. Sipping cabernet, petting and chatting with the dogs, and waiting for me.

On September 30, I had had a free afternoon, and I remembered it because the final appointment of the day, which ended at 1:30 p.m., had been a particularly grueling session with a borderline personality case I hadn't treated for much longer than that. I had gone to Fresh Market in Pleasant Ridge and shopped for the really good ingredients, carefully choosing everything, trying to take my mind out of the patient's mind and put it into an evening with my wife. I had texted her, "ritzy dinner tonight." She responded that she would work from home after 3 p.m. so she would be present for its being ready. "Unless its going 2 b done b4 3? :)"

I thought about the other entries going backward in time, sweet notes about me, us, interspersed with general work fatigue and complaints. I was starting to see how little she liked her job. I thought about her rush to leave the university, how in hindsight it had been a rash mistake, one that now seemed to be secretly crippling her. She had offered it almost immediately after her confession, but I hadn't talked through it with her, as I would have with any patient, no matter how much I agreed with his or her course of action.

"She needs to return to university life," I said. The dogs both cocked their heads because I had spoken aloud. They were sitting now, but still anxiously regarding every movement I made, desperate not to miss their treats.

She hadn't spoken about general displeasure with her work, just daily details that worried at her. She also hadn't talked about other things I was beginning to pick up, her weight consciousness, her unsettled feeling at home, especially on days that I was with patients all day or most of the evening.

Catherine, short at 5'2", had always been small, probably due mostly to nervousness and a metabolism fueled by an inner anxious perfectionism. But she'd also always been athletic, as well, a dancer as a child and teenager, who morphed into a kind of gym rat in grad school, exercising or working out three or four days a week. I had never known her to weigh herself daily, but clearly by the time she was writing this volume, she was thinking about it often and measuring herself by what she considered high and low weight. Was that Robert's residual influence? He liked thin people, and even apart from him, separated from him, she wanted to be likeable, attractive, appealing to him, to her idea of him. Maybe she had assimilated his value system that completely.

I scanned to see if she had written about Tyler's death, because it seems to have impacted her. But I couldn't find an entry around that time or since dealing with it. I kept paging backwards.

I paused then on an entry from April of last year, for which she wrote several pages. Before I read all of it, I checked my own calendar. I had been at a conference in Dallas for two days about a week before this entry was dated.

April 12

> *Nice weather today. Spring is changing to summer. Warmish, not humid yet, but I can feel it coming. Hope?*
>
> *H had no clients this afternoon; I played working-from-home and came home to see him. We went down to the Arkansas River trails with the dogs and crossed the Big Dam Bridge to walk along the paths there. Remembered so vividly running with Robert there last October. Obviously, not same time of year, but same feeling of air. H wearing same color as R even. Shitty universe. Bright blue. Out of the corner of my eye, when I was futzing with L's collar, though, it was my memory of R running with me come to life. My heart leaped and was also scared, like in my dreams when I dream we are together somewhere. It's always "illegal," and we must sneak. And I was kind of scared, like I was when H and I went to Chicago for the long weekend in February and I thought I saw R on the street ahead of us. I really thought it was him, tall lanky man, business type, salt in mostly pepper hair, trench coat. It might have been possible, and I had an instant panic and sentimental moment. Of course it wasn't. If H noticed, he said nothing. I think he has taught himself to say nothing. I reinforce/reward his silence by being sweet. Maybe we are going back to what we were before? Didn't know if I wanted to until today, because even after the blue-shirt scare, and I had calmed all those emotions down, maybe a mile later, near the soccer fields, almost to the dog park, H said something so*

sweet and kind to Wesley, who was dragging a little out of stubbornness and being out of shape. He said, "We don't want to go without you, Wesley. So join us, if you like, or we shall join you." And he said it so amazingly nicely, without any irritation or manipulation, just with love and care for that little guy, and I knew not only that I could love him, but that I did love him and will love him.

And I think I must get used to this normal that is different from my old normal before I had been in love with someone else, and this normal is that I miss something I cannot have anymore, but I have a lot, almost too much, and it is wonderful. And I can be happy and sad at the same time, and sometimes I will be happier than sad and sometimes sadder than happy, but I'm where I want *to be. And having to manage the blue-shirt moments is a consequence of what I did. And I can do it because I* want *to do it.*

I had seen this in her, this duality, and I had resented it because it meant he was on her mind, but now I saw, too, that she lived with it in order to live with me, to stay with me and remain in our family. I shut the book, feeling satiated. Feeling full.

I could not stand to sleep in our bed, and I was too hopped up on coffee, and, admittedly, the uppers and downers cycle of caffeine and alcohol with little to eat, to sleep very much at all.

• • •

During that spring when she was moving between jobs, the summer when she was consulting and traveling more, and the fall when things settled into a routine, I was distracted more than I wanted to be by thoughts of Catherine running into Robert or still seeing him somehow, but I tried not to ask her about it, tried not to act on my fear, but to act on my pretend trust.

I should have been more worried about how Tyler, Robert's 24-year-old son, and his fate were connected to mine.

After Catherine left the university, my decision to trust her was easier, and I did what I tell my clients to do: Make a daily decision to commit, to stay together, to try. Our new routines with her working downtown with more consistent office hours — her fighting the commuting traffic, working out to an exercise DVD, going to the gym or running at the River Trail before work, teleconferencing in the evening with colleagues in Chicago and Dallas — marked our new marriage with a clear milestone, and I was satisfied to look at this different stage as a change for the better. She traveled more, of course, than when she had been at the university, but she was less in charge of herself than a professor is in her daily routine. She had to report all her billable hours, and her consulting firm liked to send a team of people on almost every assignment, "to show force and commitment," she explained to me.

Of course, I thought about her opportunities with some of the men she worked with, and with her male clients, but I made a conscious decision not to bring it up too often. Sometimes, feeling vulnerable, I would confess my fears to her. She reassured me, unwaveringly.

"When you're out with your friends, you're really out with them, right?" I asked her once when she got home from cocktails with two of her former university colleagues.

"Yes, yes," she said. She watched me as she answered.

I pushed. "Do you talk about him?" I asked her, since these women had worked with him, too.

"Sometimes they mention him, in the course of things, but the effect on me...it probably isn't what you think, what you might be worried about," she said, coming over to me, trying to look into my face. Her words were clear and measured, as if she had anticipated such a question. We were on our deck then, looking out at the woods. Beyond them were more winding roads, houses, and Cantrell Road, and behind us the Arkansas River, down below, with its dark currents and wild water on windy days.

"What I think it is? What am I worried about?" I said, more to myself, turning to watch Lavinia in the grass down below us.

She answered, "Maybe you think it interests me...stirs something in me, but I have separated the person they talk about from all of that. I can hear about him and keep emotional distance. It's not painful. It's not...anything. They are speaking of him in a work way, and in that way, I am indifferent. Do you know what I mean?"

"It's not 'him' with a capital 'H' is what you're saying, when they mention him, and you listen?" I clarified for myself, and she nodded. She started to say something, looking excited, reassuring, even, but then, paused, took a breath, and when she responded, I was sure it was with a new thought that meant something else was left unsaid.

"Yes, that is what you hear me saying, doctor." She laughed, making a face as if she were in conversation with herself, and sat down in my lap, draping her arms easily around my shoulder, gazing down at Lavinia, and Wesley, who had ambled off the deck and was lying in a fading spot of sun in the grass. I smiled, but I persisted.

"What do you say, when they talk about him? Do you praise him? Remember him fondly?" She kept her arms around my neck, but I felt them stiffen. She sat up straighter, and let her eyes wander off the dogs and into the trees.

"I say what I would say about him in that work context. I can tell you don't understand what I was saying before; in that way I am indifferent. Absolutely indifferent." Her voice was insistent, annoyed, but I heard some softness for me, still. "Madeline said tonight that before he left," She was not saying his name at all. "...he denied her request for another tenure-line position in marketing. Didn't even pass it up the chain. Of course, she was irritated by that because he knew he was leaving and he took an irrevocable action that someone else, either his replacement or the dean, might have done differently. I agreed with her that it was shitty and has created problems for her, because I *do* think that, and I'm empathizing with my friend." She paused and toyed with a button on my shirt that had a chipped edge. "I just don't, I don't engage my mind or emotions in another way in those instances. I'm being *her* friend, not a woman with..."

She trailed off. Then she said, very quietly, as if it weren't for me to hear, "Indifference is the opposite of love."

"What?"

"I just said...I mean, hatred isn't the opposite of love. Indifference is. Wouldn't you agree, counselor?"

"You're talking to me as if I were litigious."

She smiled, a short, diminished smile.

I wasn't sure I could believe her; it seemed so dissociative to me, so clinically disconnected. But I couldn't stand to argue it anymore because I could see it was what she wanted to believe about herself, and probably what she thought she had to do to maintain these friendships and keep her hand in the academic world she hadn't wanted to leave.

"Did you decide where we're going out to dinner on Saturday?" She pivoted in my lap to look at the dogs, turning her face from me.

"I want us to celebrate that I'm being put on the new account. It's so much more interesting than what I've been doing."

I couldn't remember what account it was she wanted.

"You should decide then; it's your celebration," I clinked my glass to hers.

"No, I want you to plan it and surprise me, and just take me on a date."

"I will fete you appropriately," I said, but I was jealous of the excitement of the affair she must have felt compared to the mundane life we lived. "I'm sorry you have to ask for that."

Her eyebrows moved down and her mouth made a small, closed "O." "I can ask for what I want without it being an indictment...counselor." She smiled.

She returned to the old topic and I felt her legs and back tighten just a little. "I had to develop that kind of thick skin to get through the little time I had left there, initially, with classes, that kind of thing. Now I just use it whenever the topic arises. I don't want to be upset all the time."

She walked over to the deck rail and called to both the dogs. They slowly rose from their languor and ambled over to the deck stairs, moving slowly to keep their relaxed attitude up the three steps toward her, and then puddled themselves around her legs. She still was looking out at our small lawn and the trees, and she reached down to pet whoever was within reach. Lavinia stretched her shepherd head up to receive Catherine's touch. They stood like that, and my wife said no more before I got up in a few minutes to go make more gin and tonics for us before dinner.

Day Four

4

AFTER MIDNIGHT, I GAVE UP on sleeping and rose to do something to distract myself and put my nervous energy to work.

I decided to clean up the house. I had been straightening up after myself, but I hadn't been really taking care of things, and with the police in and out and the dogs bringing in the detritus of a wet Arkansas winter, the wood floors of our ranch house were feeling gritty. We had a maid service, but they only came twice a month and had most recently visited the Friday before Catherine disappeared.

I got out the Swiffer that Catherine used daily in between maid visits and noticed the attached bottle of cleaning fluid was empty, so I went into the pantry to find a replacement, hoping there was a full one. I never bought these things, and I marveled at what Catherine juggled. She had mentioned in therapy the life I made possible for her, but even in the few days since her disappearance, I was starting to notice around the house what she made possible for me, without ever mentioning it. In addition to her more than full-time job, she kept us in groceries and supplies, dealt with the mail and all our subscriptions and paid the bills. My first wife had done all this, too.

I kept a little notepad on the counter while I mopped that the police detectives had suggested I carry around in case I remembered any detail that might be important. The first page had a couple scratchings on it of what Catherine had been wearing, her last comments about work, which had been made when the detective urged me to keep the list. There had been nothing since. All I could think of was what I was keeping from them; there was no room for things I could share.

The dogs went out on the deck in the dark, and though it was cold, in the low 30s, it was a clear night, and they were relaxed and enjoying themselves, like children on a snow day, energized by the break in routine.

I mopped the floor with the Swiffer, but it still seemed grimy to me, so I got out a bucket, Mr. Clean and a few rags, found an old chair cushion, and got down on my hands and knees to scrub the floor myself.

Our house had wood floors throughout, which is one of the reasons Catherine had settled on it when we moved, leaving the house in Hillcrest I'd kept from my first marriage. I loved this new house for the deck and yard, and for its split-level in the back; After the practice I'd shared with my ex-wife and an occupational therapist dissolved, around the time of my engagement to Catherine, I wanted to be able to treat patients in a section of my home. This house had an area removed from our living space, a second level that opened to the backyard with a separate entrance, a small inner office for patient consultation, a bathroom as well as a large outer area that Catherine had ingeniously decorated to serve as both a waiting area and a secondary family area for us that we used when we hosted parties that spilled out onto the lawn. The overstuffed couches were accented with rich autumn colors, making it a soothing place for reading, or thumbing through magazines. I rarely went there to relax on my own, associating it too much with my waiting patients, but Catherine liked to go down there on the weekends or afternoons when I had no patients to sip a glass of wine, read magazines, grade or watch television with the dogs.

Our kitchen wasn't large, but it connected to a dining area that Catherine had divided into an eating area and a comfortable reading nook, where there are large windows looking out on the deck, yard and the ravine that fell away from our house down to the small, rocky stream far below.

Catherine had a penchant for turning any area that wasn't structurally dedicated to something else, like kitchen appliances or an entryway, into a "comfortable reading area." I remembered the conversations we had about putting this chair, ottoman, hanging lamp, and stacking bookshelves that served as an end table for Catherine's herb tea here in a room that should be taken up with a dining table and chairs.

"If we do what you want here, we won't have room for a dining room," I had objected as she walked about the house after our offer had been accepted. She was carrying a tape measure, and her phone, which she used to note all the dimensions she was coming up with for each room.

"And we need a dining room for...?"

"Well, what people use dining rooms for, dinner parties."

"Who's going to cook for these dinner parties we won't be able to have?" She winked at me. She could cook, but hated to do it. It was the one defect in her Southernness, as she was a thoughtful and gracious hostess, the friend who would make you a gift bag for your big meeting and always had cut flowers on the coffee table. I liked cooking but was a consistent failure at it, beyond anything day to day. I was too impatient for multistep processes, or to time out various courses or dishes to be done in stages. When I cooked for our dinner, we ate when it was ready, and Catherine had often joked when she walked in the door after work that I could start cooking, because of all the times food had been finished before she arrived and had to be reheated in the microwave. "The world's most impatient therapist," she used to call me when she realized that once I started making something, I just wanted to finish it, no matter what the clock said or what the schedule was.

"We'll need to have people over sometimes," I said. "And won't we want to eat in here ourselves occasionally?"

"We can! We'll have a small four-top right here." She gestured toward the large window. "It'll be like a beautiful restaurant! The view!" She was looking out at the trees and sky. In the spring, when the trees were full of leaves, we couldn't see our counterparts across the ravine from the back of our house. "But it's a restaurant just for us." She came over to me, and hugged me, and kissed me, not sweetly, but sensuously, lingeringly. I held her hard and returned her kiss. She had seemed finally happy with her academic position and the house, the future.

So we hadn't had dinner parties, but we had hosted things, and her comfortable-chairs fetish had helped to offset the kitchen-dwelling phenomenon that occurs at most gatherings. Our first party, we had wandered throughout the house, finding little groups of people in most of the rooms. She had been so pleased, and also had worn a slightly triumphant look, daring me to bring it up so she could utter some form of "I told you so."

I had been sitting in this very chair after the last person had left that night, finishing a beer, when she walked in, and asked, "May I come in and talk it over?" I looked up, surprised by such explicit deference. She had laughed when she saw my face. "I'm quoting *Age of Innocence*! Winona Ryder asks Daniel Day-Lewis that after their big dinner party."

I had known she meant the movie, not the book. She was a voracious reader, but not of literature, or much fiction at all, really. She read in her field, and also a lot of popular management books. She loved biographies, history, popular psychology, trending topics like "crowd sourcing" and anything by Malcolm Gladwell. I had never seen her read any of the books of the movies she loved so much, *Age of Innocence, The English Patient, Never Let Me Go.* When friends gave her the books of films she was raving about, she didn't even try to get into them. She'd give them away or donate them to book stores or put them in friends' rummage sales.

She was pleased that night, and said she was starting to feel like she was "a real grown up." "We have friends! They came over! They had fun!" She was a little tipsy, happy, not drunken. Maybe taking the UALR job was a good choice after all. She knew people here. She was known.

"Does this make you feel more like we are together more than just moving in? We hosted a party?" I asked.

"Maybe. It's different." She considered, happily, looking almost like she had something delicious in her mouth, delighted in her mulling.

This room had been a happy place for me since that night. I almost always thought of her smile and quiet but warm satisfaction after that party when I came in here. Sometimes, I had set our dinner table in here when I cooked for her because of the sense I had of this room, a place where she had not only been joyful, but also satisfied with the outcome of something that had made her anxious. She did have a community here. They would come over. She could create a nice time for them. In a new place, she would have had to start over.

These things that had brought me happiness with Catherine, the memories that sustained me through my hurt and anger over the affair, were now the softest points in my psyche, the most open spaces to wounds, from outside and from within.

I dropped the rag and towels and went looking for where I had left the scotch bottle and glass. I continued working all night, but my efforts became more and more lackadaisical the more I drank. The dogs came in and out and followed me, or didn't, or they lay on the deck. Every time they came inside, though, they would walk throughout the house, going upstairs, looking for Catherine.

At 7:30 a.m., after I had worked all night, the doorbell rang. I expected the police, bringing something back or coming to pick up something else, and I felt a wave of panic: How would it look that I just scrubbed the house from wall to wall? Was I losing all rational decision-making ability? I threw the cleaning supplies as quickly as I could in the entryway closet, but knew it would take almost no inspection to catch what I had done.

Instead, I found Sandra, my ex-wife, bundled on the porch. Even though I'd vaguely expected her, I didn't immediately open the door for her to walk in; she'd never been in the house I shared with Catherine.

"I won't stay," she said in response to my blocking the doorway to the warm living room, seating and a longer talk. I returned her gaze, though not the rather typical therapist's comforting look she was shooting at me.

For a therapist, I found Sandra to be one of the least empathetic people I knew. She was more like a coach than a counselor, pushing people one way or another, instead of helping them see where they wanted to go. I used to think it was the medical training, but the longer I was away from her, the more I saw that it was just her.

"I just, you know, I saw—" Sandra uncomfortable. This was new. "I saw the news, the paper, and I'm sorry. I'm very sorry for you, and I hope she comes home soon."

I felt a wave of unexpected emotion, a desire to confide in her, even while I knew it was a tactical error, that it wouldn't end well, that she was only being friendly-but-not-friends to me. Instead of answering her when I didn't trust myself, I looked out at Kingwood as a dark sedan slid by.

"Did you hear what I said?" she asked.

"How many times during our marriage did you ask me that?" It was meant as an accusation, but she took it as a rib.

"Well, let's not count. Counting's a sign of a problem," she said, poking fun at herself, our profession. "Can I do anything for you? I suppose I can't imagine what, but I wanted to offer."

"I'm having a lot of trouble sleeping," I answered, looking her in the face.

"I thought you might be," she said, reaching in her bag. "I brought some samples of different things. I know I can trust you not to overuse..."

"Obligatory disclaimer?"

I put my hand out and she deposited the colorful pharma boxes in my palm.

"I wouldn't mind a prescription," I said, still bald, without shame.

She nodded, and dug in her anorak's pocket for a prewritten order, handing it to me without a word.

I was about to let her in, but she seemed to dig in as she spoke again.

"I know you love her, and I know this is hard for you." She was making herself look at me, but her eyes were darting from my gaze so much, I looked back into the street, following her glances. She was my height, with black, not brown, short hair, physically thicker than Catherine, probably just due to age, or maybe because she'd had her child late in life. Her red anorak-style parka cinched at the waist with some kind of technical widget. This was very Sandra. She was very seriously sporty. She was intensely anything she did.

"I hope she knows that, wherever—" I stopped myself. This was dangerous. I could confide too much in just a heartbeat more.

"You know what I say, right? It's in my book?" I shook my head, preoccupied with censoring my desire to use her as some kind of confessor, there in the cold with the house empty of Catherine behind me.

"You can't know if someone loves you," she said, looking at me, unblinking. "You can only know if you feel loved."

I declined to ask her how she felt about me; I knew the answer. As I thanked her for the pills and she assured me that I could call her for any other assistance, I felt the physical discomfort that comes with unsettling thoughts. Catherine had chosen me and our marriage instead of her relationship with Robert, probably for many complex reasons, but I could not be sure that she did so because she felt loved.

• • •

With Catherine's disappearance, I became more and more afraid that these last months, heavy with grief and tinged, still, with bitterness and suspicion, might have been our last times together. My trust in her had been shallow, the coating on glass that makes a mirror, instead of something deep or love-fueled, because my forgiveness of her was only skin-deep.

The harbinger of what was ahead for her, for me, turned out to be a strange news item in the Arkansas *Democrat-Gazette* in September, just after Labor Day. In the Arkansas section, there was a short article, three paragraphs, about Robert's middle son, Tyler, and how he died after his car hit one of the late-night trains running through the Riverdale neighborhood of Little Rock. He was alone, and police were examining evidence indicating he had been drinking.

I read the article two or three times, trying to find something to make contact with that would explain the vague, inchoate emotional reaction I was having. *It's just Robert, just things related to Robert,* I told myself. I saw the dogs looking at me and realized I had said that aloud.

I wasn't sure how to tell Catherine about Tyler, or even if I should tell her. She didn't read the paper, but the question was made irrelevant by her former UALR colleague, who texted the news to her while she was driving to work. Five minutes after I read the article, she called. I saw her name on my cellphone, and I knew she knew.

"Catherine?"

"I just heard something...Tyler was killed," she said. Her voice wasn't firm, but she didn't sound like she was crying. Just shaken.

"I saw it in the paper. It sounds like he was drinking and ran into a train. That never ends well." I was grateful she was talking to me about it, that I was her go-to call, not Robert. But it was also specifically awful to sympathize with her that her ex-lover's son had died.

"I just got a text," she said. "I don't know much of what happened. He was pretty mixed up, but this is just terrible. And..."

"Yes?"

"I'm just, I'm sorry. It's okay if you don't want to talk about it. I—"

"It's all right. Just talk to me." I could hear her breathing, which sounded a little like she was crying now. "Did you know him at all?" I asked, steeling myself for the answer. I knew so little about her and Robert, how they were together, what their relationship included, what it was like. I wanted to know, and I did not want to know, and the anxiety always bested the curiosity in me when it came up. Now, though, I wanted to understand my wife, even if later I regretted it.

"No, no," she answered immediately. "He worked for about a minute at the university, but I only knew who he was. He did..." She stopped. Took a breath. "Sorry, but he did seem to know who I was, or was suspicious of who I was. I think he saw us, once, walking back from lunch. I don't know. Robert said something about it and was uncomfortable with it. I guess he suspected something, but I can't remember. I don't know if that was before..."

"To my thinking, there is nothing 'before.' It's all part of it."

She finished, "I'm sorry. I don't know how to...It's just...it's just, it's an awful way for someone to die. And I knew him, even though I am not supposed to have, or...something like that. I shouldn't have called you." She said the last sentence as if it were a question.

"It's all right, Catherine. I saw the news story, and it shook me up a little, too. I'm not sure why, either. It's all right. Just...just try to have a good day, and come home to me, and we'll be together."

"Thank you so much," she whispered. Now she was crying.

Over the next few days, I searched out what I could about Tyler's death, but not when Catherine was around. Between patients the next day, I read a longer story in the paper; a beat reporter had made the connection between Tyler and his father, and pursued the story.

"Son of Venture Capital Fund Guru Killed In Train Collision," read the headline.

The article continued:

> Tyler Gewinn, 24, son of ARKFUND President and CEO Robert Gewinn, was killed early Wednesday morning when the pickup truck he was driving collided with a train as the locomotive crossed Riverdale Avenue south of the Riverdale-Cantrell intersection, near Jessie Drive.
>
> There are currently no identified witnesses. The pickup truck, registered to Robert Gewinn, is believed to have hit the train head-on, having broken through the barrier arms, which were lowered to warn of the train's crossing, according to Little Rock Police Spokesman Barry Esser.
>
> "From our examination of the scene and computer logs of signals and train communications, we are confident the safety systems in place were properly activated," said Esser in a statement.
>
> The police report noted several empty or partially empty alcohol bottles in the totaled pickup cab, as well as drug paraphernalia. Toxicology reports on Tyler Gewinn are not expected until next week or later. Tyler was identified as the driver of the vehicle. No passengers were listed.
>
> Tyler's father, Robert Gewinn, 62, was named in April as the Director and CEO of the high-profile ARKFUND, a venture capital firm based in Little Rock funded by a mix of Arkansas public development monies and private investment firms, such as Smithson and Crane Partners. Robert Gewinn was previously

assistant dean of the School of Business at UALR, where he focused on the university's entrepreneur programs and incubator efforts.

Robert Gewinn and his wife of 35 years, Petra Welsh Gewinn, have two surviving sons, Robert Jr., "Robbie," 27, of Fayetteville, and Joshua, 20, of Little Rock. Robert Gewinn could not be reached for comment.

Tyler Gewinn was unemployed at the time of his death. He attended UALR for two years following his graduation from Arkansas Christian Academy for Boys, and had been employed at UALR, Elk Cleaners and, most recently, Cable Comm in the Little Rock area as a sales associate. He leaves no other survivors.

Googling the story brought no further information, and television news stories online were devoid of greater detail. I cleared my browser history after each search.

Catherine didn't speak about it anymore after that night, when she seemed less emotional and more guarded about her feelings than she had been when she called me. I did ask her about what she knew about him, because I felt she wanted to talk through it more. Discussing him personally seemed a safer course to follow, and I didn't ask her about how she knew what she did know about him.

We were eating outside on our deck during one of the few really glorious Arkansas fall days — after the humidity has begun to abate and before the days become rainy, gray and cold for what seems like weeks on end. Wesley and Lavinia had given up on getting anything from our plates and were down on the grass, Wesley lying near my small herb garden; Lavinia patrolling the perimeter, but keeping an eye and an ear out for any opportunities for food from us.

Catherine had changed from her work suit to pajama pants and her ripped up red and white Roots sweatshirt she'd had since she nannied in Toronto during her undergraduate years. Her long hair was up in a lop-sided bun with the ends sticking straight up as they did when she straightened her hair and killed all the waves and curls I liked so much. She had on her pink knit house shoes over Smartwool striped socks. She poured glasses of wine for both of us.

"Red doesn't go with shrimp, but I wanted something meaty," she said, topping off my glass with the rest of the bottle. "Do we have more?"

"I think that may be it, but I'll run up to Sullivant's for you or over to Yancey's, if you want. I need to pick up something to give to Nikki to thank her for proofing that article for me, and I could drop it off on the way home."

"Nikki," she said. "She is the world's funniest therapist. She should be a comedian. Also, it's 'wine day' at Yancey's. Fifteen percent off."

I wondered if Catherine sounded jealous, but I didn't ask. The night was too nice. She was too happy. I was enjoying acting happy.

"I could come with you," she said, stretching out her arms to demonstrate her attire, and then laughing slightly. "I could get dressed."

"No, no, I may not even go," I said. "I just wanted to offer. I know you had an emotional day," and with that I had opened the door for her. If she walked through it, I would follow behind. I would follow if she would be careful about what she said, how she said it.

"He was messed up," she said, letting her voice trail off. She was watching Lavinia navigate the fence, where it intersected the garden.

"You said that," I prompted. "What do you mean? On drugs? Criminally?"

"I don't know about criminally," she answered. She was looking down, and to the right, which she did when she was carefully considering what she would say and wanted no distractions. "Maybe he was by now, but before" — what an ominous word, I thought, *before* — "he drank a lot and, he did some drugs. He gambled, too, and lost all of the money he had inherited from his grandfather — I guess all the boys got some, and it was a lot — too much for boys. He didn't hold on to jobs very well.

"And that whole post-Christian Academy scene..."

"Yeah, some of those guys don't ever really grow up," I agreed. I'd gone to Central High School and had watched the products of that private school my whole life, in high school, in college, in their careers.

"They're...funny, you know, peculiar, aren't they?" she agreed.

"Some guys thrive in that environment, that 'we'll make you a man' thing."

"Is that what it is? Is that what they do?" She stuck her chin out and with the under bite, absently gnawed at her upper lip. "But that implies, doesn't it, that there is one way to be a man," she observed.

"I think that's what they believe. I mean, what else can they promise to deliver if they don't have a fixed point in mind?"

She started to answer, but then looked out toward the dogs and her face went blank.

The private system was a staple of Little Rock society, at all levels, which felt like a good thing, the diversity, the mixing of economies and populations in the hallways, and given Little Rock's historical issues with public education, its private schools were influencers in the city. Their superintendents and headmasters were always at the big meetings, at the leadership tables. And Little Rock's particular brand of Southern Evangelism mixed with its role as a liberal pocket in an increasingly red state made this high school a melting pot of those fleeing public schools for almost as many reasons as there were children enrolled. But once in the boys' high school, they were all bullets aimed at the same target, to become upstanding, straight, white, conventionally male breadwinning alumni. Only a small percentage of the students came from the rarefied worlds the students were being were aimed at, by their parents, by the teachers and coaches. An equally small percentage hit that target, but it wasn't always the same boys who came in privileged and met that level of success in the end. I knew the students, I'd worked with the alumni...and I had treated them, and their wives and children, too.

I confessed that I had read the newspaper article, but if she noticed what it cost me to do so, she didn't show it. "The reporter referenced alcohol and drugs," I pointed out.

"Yes," she said, "I noticed that. He hadn't ever been to rehab or anything like that that I know of, but of course, I don't know everything about him then, and nothing about him now. I suppose that might have been the best thing for him. Well, better than this." She sipped at her wine, without irony, stretching out the last drops.

"What about the jobs? The paper said he worked at UALR. You said that, too, this morning," and as soon as I said it, I had taken the lead, and was walking ahead of her down this dangerous path.

She looked up at me, gauging my toughness, perhaps, assessing how much she could share. I turned my head toward Lavinia. "What is she doing? Is she in the dirt?" I stood.

"She is, but she's not digging or anything. She's just standing there. She likes that spot, because just there, she can see to the side yard where the Hinsons' yard touches ours, and their little dachshunds."

I handed her my half-full glass of wine, and she took it without remarking, without thanking me, even. She took a healthy drink and then looked at me again carefully, sat, and decided to answer my previous question full on. I knew she was going to before she spoke. She was sitting forward on her chair, and she moved her shoulders back-and-down, as she did anytime she was putting herself to something that made her nervous. I'd gotten the habit from her.

"Robert got him the job at the university, even though you're not really supposed to be able to do that, with all the checks on state government employment among family members," she answered. The name stung even though I knew she was going to say it. I let her feel her way forward, take the lead back from me. "He could do that for him because it wasn't completely a UALR department, but it was on the campus and Robert was not the direct boss of the supervisor, but he was kind of a de facto boss of the whole initiative because he had written the grant ten years ago that funded the whole thing — or he had gotten the grant written."

"Was Tyler qualified for the job?" I asked, reflexively focusing her on the son, not the father. "The article said he went to UALR for only two years."

"Yeah, that was a stretch," she answered quickly. "He went for maybe three semesters, and he dropped and failed a lot of classes, but the job was kind of pre-entry level, really. I think it was originally approved as an internship, but..." she trailed off.

"Is that how you knew him?"

"I knew he had worked there," she said, delicately. The injection of the word "had" was a subtle reinforcement that his employment on campus took place before her affair had started. "Everyone in the college knew he'd had trouble and knew his parents," she looked down as she said those words, "were worried about him, were trying to get him back into a university environment."

She grimaced to herself, an expression both of empathy and concern. She took another drink.

"And I mean, I just felt sorry for him. Any screw up like that is kind of a pitiable thing, you know? But in his case, the contrast among brothers was really clear. His older brother was in pharmacy school. His younger brother had a full scholarship to Hendrix and was studying some esoteric, self-created major in philosophy and the arts, and Tyler was just, you know. Well, you know, the newspaper description, though it was brief, was pretty complete — based on my experience, I mean, I guess..."

"Sometimes there isn't more to say," I said.

"Yes," she said, examining my face to see if I wanted to stop her from saying more. Her eyes looked up into mine, and held them. I returned her gaze.

"Is this okay?" she asked.

"Fuck it," I said. "Let's just talk about it and then move on."

She nodded. "He couldn't keep the job, and I don't think he wanted to. He didn't always come in, or he was late, or he wouldn't do the little bit of work he was given, filing, correspondence, summarizing information, that kind of thing," she said. "He lasted less than three months, I think. He quit though, but he was about to get fired. They would have fired him sooner, I think, but, well, you know. Then he did the same thing at that Elk Cleaners on Reservoir, though he seems to have gotten that job himself."

"He worked at a radio station? Ad sales? Something like that?" I prompted. My professional curiosity had been engaged, somewhat against my will.

"Not a radio station," she said. "At Cable Comm's in Little Rock." There was a surprising note of enthusiasm in her voice. "He went from Elk to Cable Comm somehow, and Robert did not know how he did it. Robert didn't get him the job or ask for a favor or anything."

"Catherine—" I protested, automatically, almost robotically. She was too comfortable now.

"Sorry. I'm sorry. I am..." I told her to go on, and she did, careful again, but still taken by her subject. "It just was such a strange thing, that they would hire him from behind the counter where he worked — when he bothered to show up — for a white-collar job that's kind of detail oriented and professional. It lasted a little longer than the others, maybe six months. So strange..." she trailed off, taken with her memories.

"Addicts often have periods of positive activity and getting their acts together," I said. "Then they plummet again if they aren't coping with the real problems, facing up to them. The article said he was unemployed."

"It ended last November," she said. "Right after Thanksgiving. He'd been living at home, and there had been some hope he would find a place, but then there wasn't." About this knowledge, as with several other facts this evening, I did not ask the source. Her language was adroitly vague. She might mean she had kept tabs on him, or that her day-to-day knowledge of his life expired when her affair did.

I took the glass of wine I'd given her back and drank the last third in a gulp.

"I guess you're going to Yancey's!" she said.

"You know," I said, holding up the empty glass and gathering up the empty bottle and her drained glass, "Addictions run in families."

"Yes." This was all she said. She was watching Lavinia again, who had started to come up the deck stairs, sensing we might be at an end of our dinner outside. "Yes."

"Petra?" I remembered her declining drinks more often than accepting them. Maybe she was sober now.

"No, I don't think so. I guess I don't know, but well...Robert drank too much. Honestly. Even at work things that were off campus. It was...it could be bad."

"I did not know that," I said, almost to myself. I was turned away from her then, as she walked toward Lavinia, and I didn't think she heard me. She had found, then, a nonjudgmental drinking companion in her lover, I thought. She drank more than I did, and she was sensitive to my feelings about it.

"How could you? Well, I mean, I guess we did socialize some, but I think he was on good behavior around you, and around Petra, too. But he definitely had a problem. I'm not the only one who saw it," she said, a little petulantly, defensively.

"I believe you." I meant my tone to be reassuring, but if it was, she was feeling too exposed or vulnerable to hear it.

"I'm just trying not to tap into too many things I know because of all the awfulness," she said, pausing. "The affair, and so I, I am just saying that people saw it. That's why some people said it was good he left UALR. That flashy venture capital world is a lot better fit for that kind of habit. Campus life can be a bit puritanical, at least on the administrative side, especially in Arkansas."

I sat down beside her, and put my arm around her. "Well, you certainly dress more puritanically now than you did when you worked there," I said. "You know, you wear those suits you say are the suits men would wear if they were women."

She smiled, "I stole that line from *Working Girl*," she admitted.

"I know," I said.

"You knew? You always laugh when I say it, as if you're impressed with my wit!"

"I am impressed with your wit. I'm impressed with a lot of things about you." I kissed her temple. Lavinia put her dirty paws on Catherine's pajama-clad legs, but she didn't brush her off. She just reached out and began squeezing her ear and petting it with one hand.

We had finished talking about Tyler, but I had found out something she didn't like about Robert, and I had found out more about his son, and I was breaking my own rule about hazarding professional guesses about people I didn't know well or had never treated.

This had been a warning, missed and misunderstood.

• • •

"Robert Gewinn, please." I told the assistant my name. Her tone was discouraging. She didn't know who I was, ergo, her boss would not have time for me. But she returned to the line and enthusiastically put me through.

"What can I do for you? Have you had news?" He sounded professional, but unsettled, too, eager.

"I wouldn't call you with news about Catherine. You're not a family member," I said, pausing, but he was silent. "I'm calling you because you lied to me at the bridge yesterday." I was trying to undo how foolish I felt for believing him at all.

He was silent for a few breaths, and I wondered if he was about to hang up. I was ready to redial when I felt the line go dead, but then he spoke slowly, and very, very carefully.

"What did I lie to you about?"

"You've seen her," I said, equally considered, equally careful.

Another pause, but now I knew he would not hang up. "I didn't see the point of — of — giving you something to be angry with her for. I assume you're talking about the School of Business luncheon last fall?" His voice went up in pitch when he asked the question; had he gambled too much with this specific truth? He returned to a more even tone. "How did you find out about that?"

"I cannot fucking believe you didn't tell me you were trying to warn Catherine."

"Have they found her?" Now I could hear real hope and relief in his voice.

"No, they haven't found her. They won't find her either with you keeping things to yourself, things we need to know to find her. What were you warning her about?" I was practically screaming into the phone, sitting in my office, where I was now acting like the patients I most disliked.

He inhaled and I thought he would speak, and then he didn't.

"Robert...come on."

"I heard what you said about not wanting things about our affair to come out. I agree with you. I don't want that either. Not for me, of course, or my wife, my sons, you or Catherine. I don't know that what I said to her has anything to do with the case anyway. It could just be some kind of red herring."

"You are such a narcissistic ass!" I said, as my anger stopped flaring and became concentrated, cold. I spoke in a low tone, as if to an idiot. "Stop protecting yourself. What were you trying to warn her about? And why didn't you fucking tell her what the danger was instead of just freaking her out and leaving her vulnerable? Did you even tell her what to watch out for? Anything specific?"

"I want to talk to you about this," he said, returning my low, patronizing tone, note for note. "I do. I will. But I cannot do it here, and I don't think you're in a place to be able to take some things in. I don't think there is anything even to it. But I will tell you what I was talking to her about, and you can decide what you want to do. I just...if you're going to tell the police, to make it public, just give me some warning, please. Not for me, but for my family. We've been through a lot this year. It's just so hard on Petra. Dredging all this back up will be painful. I'd like to prepare her."

My first instinct was to talk to him where I had seen him before, to go over everything there, now that I knew more. But that would be stupid. If we were seen again together there — if we had been seen before, or noticed on surveillance camera footage — a second meeting would certainly provoke the police detectives and nullify any good luck I was having in those quarters. Before I could ask about when or where, he suggested we run into each other at the Heights Starbucks around 8 a.m. the next morning, a Saturday. I agreed, and before I could say goodbye, he hung up.

Day Five

5

I WAS ALREADY SITTING at a table when Robert got to Starbucks. I hadn't gone out much, and wasn't pleased about doing so, but no one seemed to recognize or notice me. My photo had been in the paper once so far, just a small, professional mug shot. But I overheard a couple leaving talking about Catherine's disappearance. I was glad they were stepping through the door as a phrase "not safe anywhere in this city...that poor woman on the path..." drifted back to me. Before I'd gotten out of my car, I'd taken two Xanax; my hands were shaking with adrenaline and exhaustion.

He ordered and came to sit with me, playing a little bit of the role, telling me he was sorry, could he sit down, pulling over a chair. I had sat in a nook, facing the windows on Kavanaugh, and he moved the chair near enough to speak as if we were chatting in church, low and reverential. I thought it looked odd, but I said nothing. The morning light from the street was glaring in my eyes, but seated next to me, somehow he was in shadow. I was wearing a pullover Catherine had given me and a T-shirt, and I was cold sitting close to the windows and the street, so I wrapped my scarf around my neck, but I didn't put my coat back on. I was saving that gesture in case I needed him to leave.

They called his name for his coffee, a double Americano. He turned fluidly, got up to retrieve the cup, and returned.

"I don't know what you know about my son, Tyler," he said, looking at the floor. His mouth drew down at the corners when he said his dead son's name.

"Just a little. Catherine—" It was so painful to say her name to him. I kept trying to keep all the nerve endings in my skin from cutting knifelike through the surface. I took a breath. "Catherine and I talked a little about him when he...died." He was silent. I said, "She said he had trouble sticking with things." Why was I making protective understatements for him?

"He had a lot of problems," he said, baldly. He looked me full in the face. His body language was open, not tense or wary. Chest broad. Both feet on the ground, knees straight ahead, pointed at me. Arms down at his sides, not crossed. He was prepared for this conversation, had probably scripted it between yesterday's telephone call and now.

"I had gotten Tyler the job at UALR, pulled strings, what have you. People do it," he gestured in an exculpatory manner. I nodded impatient, with his need to validate. "But he quit before he got fired. That was typical for him. He isn't...wasn't...a worker. I don't know why he was so different from his brothers, but he was.

"Well, I know one reason. He was an addict, and he always wanted the easy way to the hard thing to get. He saw the features of success, but he never understood its ways." He paused, but his manner seemed prepared, rehearsed, like he'd said this speech before. I took a gulp of my black coffee, needing the caffeine to focus.

"He was addicted to alcohol, to various drugs, to gambling. We had tried rehab — he went once, and another time he was scheduled to go, but wouldn't. And we couldn't make him. It wasn't court-ordered, and he was 18 by then. He'd get a job during a better period, and then regress and lose it or quit. College was out of the question, we could see that from miles away."

He anticipated my question. "We're pretty sure his problems started in high school, Christian Academy for Boys. I went there and thought it was good for me in the end. But he was never very high achieving, and even though we sent him to what we thought was a pretty safe private school, he found one guy, Justin Keller, who was, I don't know, a 'burnout.' Did drugs, and then sold drugs. Of course, he drank. Lots of the boys did, but, you know, serious drinking. During his junior year, Tyler confessed his drug usage to me in order to get me to pay his 'friend,' the drug dealer."

I felt like I was sitting in my office. I wished I were, because I wanted to call on that therapeutic power and authority, and I wanted the corresponding indifference — the feeling for the patient, not with, and sometimes not even for. Robert, while seeming vulnerable to me, was in complete control of this conversation.

"That guy, Keller, went on to be a real low-life, really bad news. I'm not sure if we have the mob here, or 'organized crime,' per se, but if we do, he's in it, and big in it, even though he's still young. The more I heard about him as the boys aged, the more I wished Tyler didn't know him at all. He's a murderer. At the very least."

"How do you know that?"

"I don't know it, I mean, for a fact. I just mean I'm sure he's capable of it, and if he hasn't killed someone yet, he will."

"And Tyler?"

"I assume he had other incidents like this where he owed money for the wrong things to the wrong people, and, honestly, I suspect, my wife has bailed him out as well, we probably all have, including his brothers." I was uncomfortable with the reference to his wife. Anything that evoked the marriages that had been violated seemed off-limits to me. He didn't gesture or hesitate though; he played by his own rules.

"What does this have to do with Catherine?"

"Well, I am not sure, but Tyler had issues and problems, and money troubles, and he did not like your wife."

The words, "your wife" hit me like a slap. I almost got up to leave but the words had knocked the wind out of me. Was it disdainful? Was it purposeful distance?

"Yes, she was my wife," I said in a kind of strangled stage whisper. "Not some workplace piece of ass."

He looked surprised and taxed, as he might when dealing with someone distasteful and gauche whom he wasn't allowed to correct, and paused. He took a sip of his Americano, his first since he had been seated.

I asked him, "Does your wife know you're here?"

Again, he looked pained; this feeling of not being able to correct and chastise those in his presence must be unusual for him.

"Does Petra know you're here?" I used her name on purpose.

"No. No."

"Gewinn, what's going on?"

"I want to answer that question. But I'm not positive how or if this fits together."

I met his gaze.

"I don't think Tyler died by accident, though it was entirely plausible that he would die as he did." He paused. He was not cavalier with those words. "I'm quite sure he owed money to Justin, and to someone else, for drugs, for gambling, for who knows what, and he wasn't able to pay them."

"Did he ask you for the money?"

"No. Or Petra, and I don't think his brothers either. Not this time."

"Why didn't he want to come to you, or your family, for help?"

"I don't know. Honestly, I can't understand it." For the first time that morning, Robert seemed authentically introspective. "He had come to us for money before, and it always worried me that he was *not* more sensitive to that. He was so lacking in pride where that was concerned. He just did not care about getting us to cover his gambling and drugs debts. He was never responsible, never connected the consequences with his choices to do whatever he wanted.

"All our boys had a small part of a — well, a meaningful inheritance from their grandfather, Petra's father, when they were in their teens and got it at 18. I would have changed it for him if I could have modified the trust, and I tried, but I couldn't. Robbie and Josh still have almost all of theirs. Tyler's was gone in two months, and it only lasted that long because he won a little money when he gambled with it, but then he lost it all — or spent it all on drugs."

"But this time? He didn't come to you for money?" I wasn't this interested in Tyler.

"Maybe I'm just making it up, but I found it hard to believe he would crash into a moving train when the traffic arms were down, the warning bells were ringing, and the train was going through the intersection."

"If he was out of control? Drunk or high? Or both?" I probed. *Or afraid of someone,* I thought.

"I know. I know. You can't put anything awful out of reach of a junkie." Here his tone shifted, he was speaking hypothetically, in general, not about Tyler. "But I had talked to him on the phone about 30 minutes before the accident, and he did not sound drunk. He sounded tense. Not drunk. In fact, he sounded pretty sober, and I would notice. Because he didn't always sound that way, and I remember quite clearly, because I was both worried about what was on his mind and relieved that he wasn't high."

"How did that sound? What did you talk about?"

"He was angry. You know he knew about Catherine and... me." For the first time today he sounded sincerely penitent, sensitive to my feelings, not just to appropriate behavior's demands.

"Go on," I prompted him.

"He 'suspected,' I should say. He worked at UALR before anything... anything happened, but I guess he was around me with her enough to be uncomfortable."

"How inconvenient."

"I'm sorry. I'm trying to tell you what you want to know, but I know it's, it's — painful. I don't know how to tell this story without that."

"Just go on."

He nodded. "Anyway, he was suspicious, and he didn't like her, before there was anything to dislike her for."

"Wait...did you tell your family about your affair?" I asked, flummoxed. As a therapist, I had typically taken a hard line against sharing the messy vagaries of marriages, either those ending or those staying together, with children in the family, whatever their ages. Even if it was the match to a flammable marriage, the harbinger of the end.

"I didn't. Petra did."

I had forgotten his wife was an actor in this drama, too. She had always seemed so gray and backgrounded in every situation, so passive.

"When Catherine told me she was going to tell you about it, and that it had to end, I was... I don't know... I wanted to feel for my marriage what she felt toward yours."

I opened my mouth to ask him about how it had ended, for more detail. I felt hungry to know for sure that Catherine had left him for me, but I was afraid to ask, to expose my vulnerability. My hatred surged. I picked up my now cold coffee and drank instead. I looked around the Starbucks. We were still the only ones in this corner, but a coffee klatch of men seemed to be forming at combined tables in the middle of the cafe.

"So, I went home the same night and told Petra. I didn't even have to say who it was. She knew. She'd known for a long time. She had been observant and suspicious, probably since before it even started." I moved in my seat, restless legs. He changed course.

"But we talked it out; I told her it was over. I wanted to stay, and I would do what she asked or needed in order to give us another real go. She said she wanted me to stay — of course, she was angry. She was very angry. We had some real blowouts, and some periods, days even, of not talking at all. But I always felt she wanted me to stay. Honestly, I think she wanted to win, to beat Catherine. If we split up, I think Petra would have felt she had to concede a point. She doesn't easily do that."

I, too, had a wife who conceded very few points.

"But in a moment of weakness, when things were very bad and uncertain between us, when she felt one-down, so to speak, she told our sons to get a point back at me. Tyler, of all of them, of course, reacted with the least maturity."

"What does maturity mean to you?" I asked. It was a reflex, this probing, when people used words on an assumption that their meanings were mutually agreed upon.

Robert answered, humoring me, yet still seeming authentic, maybe even enjoying the therapist's attention — they all do in the end, especially people like Robert, who pretend they don't need a thing from people, but who can't function without someone's gaze upon them. "I don't mean cynicism, if that's what you're trying to get to." I was silent, making no gesture, expressing nothing. "I mean, he didn't seem to have the capacity to imagine his parents' marriage as a marriage instead of either an idealized state or a total disaster."

I wondered if he were quoting someone else, someone like me.

"His brothers were upset, of course, but they checked in on both of us, though more on their mother. Tyler, though. Tyler..." He trailed off as his eyes fixed in a thousand-yard stare out the window and across the street to the privacy fence opposite. He corrected, squared himself after a second. "Tyler wasn't really like that. He was always so black and white. I was wrong. I was awful. His mother was a saint. She should have what she wanted. And at the same time, our family was fake. He was incredibly sensitive to the idea that this was a secret. He kept saying that, 'It's a secret. It's a secret.' As if somehow by keeping this family matter in the family, we had rendered him at risk to something beyond all of us."

I agreed with Tyler, but I said nothing.

"And I felt certain that Tyler was waiting to punish me. He was upset again when I got my ARKFUND job. He was offended that I could make a move, make more money after what I had done to our family. That the world didn't punish me upset him, and he attributed it to the secrecy, and called our secrecy hypocrisy."

I didn't mind by then if my silence communicated my agreement with his dead son.

"I am still angry with Petra for telling them. I felt it damaged them and didn't do anything for her in the long run. But she was hurt, and she was seeking a kind of power base in our family so that I would listen to her and do what she wanted, acknowledge her." I looked at him, eyebrows raised, my suspicions about him spouting therapeutic quotes resurfacing, and perhaps apparent from my expression.

"At any rate, the other boys were angry, but eager to keep the family together, and seemed to see a role for themselves in doing that. But Tyler, he was only angry. And he got angrier, and when good things happened to our family, it riled him. His drinking would flare. He was probably doing more drugs, too. His outbursts would be more emotional, more hurtful — when he was around, which was rare when he was upset with us.

"And because he had seen Catherine, knew who she was, I guess the pain of all of it was a little more immediate to him, and he had someone to focus his anger on — well, in addition to me. I certainly got a lot of it. He was angry with her, too, and when he heard — I'm not sure who told him because I didn't — that she had also gotten a new job, making more money than at the university, he was absolutely outraged. His self-righteousness really knew no bounds. Ironically."

"That's not unusual," I said, recalling families with addiction issues I had worked with. I started to say more, but I didn't want to give Robert any benefit, anything for free. "Self-righteousness can help people deny their, well, this is not a technical term, their asshole-itis."

He started to laugh, but stopped himself, though it wasn't joyous and his smile was weighted with regret.

"And Catherine?" I used her name to resurface the reason behind our meeting. "How is this all tied up together, with her? Why do you think she's connected to his death?" I was prepared to find that I had come here on a fool's errand. Family members of addicts, especially enablers, as Robert had been, rarely like to acknowledge the natural consequences of their loved one's addictions and often attribute them to outside forces. As narcissistic as Robert was, I was pretty sure he was used to externalizing consequences.

"As I said, Tyler was angry with me, and with Catherine, and outraged that the world would reward two 'cheaters' with money and better jobs." I thought of how Tyler would have liked to know Catherine didn't feel rewarded in her work as a consultant.

He paused while a woman came over to the newspaper rack and decided whether to buy a copy of The New York Times. After she left, he spoke again, more quietly. He started looking around him more often as he talked. The shadow across his face seemed to deepen and to exaggerate the lines in his weathering face.

"I guess I was worried for Catherine because I was not sure that he died the way it was meant to look like he died, and he was angry, and he was hanging around a lot with people who were bad for him. And he probably owed this Keller guy money, money he didn't ask me for.

"And I'm pretty sure people's lives are better if Justin Keller doesn't know their name."

That was it? I sat, glancing out the window at the occasional passerby, trying to sort out what was real or helpful information and simultaneously feeling there wasn't any reason for us to be sitting here talking at all. I felt humiliated...again.

"I've wasted my time today. This is ridiculous," I said, and stood.

He put his hand on my arm to stay me, but I jerked it off to put it through the sleeve of my suede jacket. I turned to gather my newspaper and my phone from the bench I'd been sitting on.

"Sit down, please, for one more minute." He looked around, conscious of how readable our argument might be, aware that someone in the restaurant could know him or me or both of us. I was sure he could describe everyone in the Starbucks and where they were seated, like some kind of spy.

I continued to stand. "I'm going. If you have anything else to say to me, say it now."

"I told her that day to be careful because I was sure Tyler had been killed. Tyler needed money when he died, for things he shouldn't have been doing, Tyler knew about us and he may have told some of these lowlifes he associated with about it. But—"

"But?"

He stood then and put on his coat and scarf. "But time has passed now, and I do not think anything happened to prove that my fears were justified."

I gasped and could feel my pulse pumping in my ears.

"My wife has disappeared, which you might be implying is because she was targeted by people who were following her. Is that nothing to you?"

"It's not nothing. Let's just go outside," he motioned me out the door, but his gesture was less masterful, and he didn't seem to know where to put his hand once he brought his arm down.

"I'm parked down here," I said, walking east on Kavanaugh. He followed me.

"This is bullshit, Robert. You lied to me about talking to her, you wanted to warn her so badly you followed her to the ladies' room at that luncheon, and you scared her enough that she almost broke down and called you about it." He looked surprised and hungry in a way, and I realized again that he didn't know about her journal. My steps got faster as I picked up steam. "You got me out of my house when I'm trying to stay home in case anything happens so you could tell me there isn't a connection but there might be a connection, but 'never mind. It's all fine.' Tyler's dead, Catherine's gone, but you were just overreacting."

We had reached my car, and I got out my keys. "Do you have any other horse shit you'd like to share today?" He stood still, slightly befuddled, blinking against the sun he had just recently stepped into, as if he were now uncomfortable with his height. I walked around to the driver's side and called over the top of the car to him, "No? Thanks for nothing, you offensive waste of skin."

• • •

Robert knew more than he was telling me, and he had been afraid enough to approach Catherine publically, but too nervous or self-protective to tell her everything she needed to know. He was doing the same thing with me. I sat in the driver's seat of my car, frozen with rage and helplessness. Even now, it was possible he had the key to her rescue — or her whereabouts — and he was keeping it to himself.

But I had a name. Justin Keller. I could tell the police. Maybe it matched up with who they were already looking for. If Robert knew so much about him, he was probably well-known to them.

I put the key in the ignition, but my hand was shaking, and I had to lower my arm down to my side and rest my hand in my lap. I massaged it with the other hand, trying to focus on something and calm myself down. I tried again and with my other hand holding my wrist, I was steady enough to get the key in and start the car. I began driving downtown to the precinct on Markham. My thoughts were inchoate and vague, and yet I felt I needed to do something to get Robert to talk — if not to me, then to the detective. They would make him talk.

As I drove toward the Kavanaugh-Cantrell intersection, my adrenaline ebbed a bit. If I went there and told the police, her affair with Robert would be a matter of public record — it would only be a matter of time. Even if they kept it quiet now, in order to pursue the thread, if there was a trial, it would all come out. Even if they didn't release the information right away to the media, it would be there, lurking, and if Robert knew who the attackers were, he would be involved in the case, which still left me nauseated. The story would be about him.

I thought about calling Brooke first, going to her office, but I didn't even know where it was. She had always come to me. I could tell everything to her, and she would know how to proceed. Or I could start with Chuck.

But the current of my feeling moved against it; I pushed back against them partly because I knew now they were the last two people to judge Catherine and me, to assess our marriage. What should have made them more available to me was making me more stubborn in my secret. Knowing what I did about them, I wanted them to know my marriage had cracked, that there were breaks in its foundations, even less than I had before.

Of course, then I would have to explain how I knew to talk to Robert about his vague warning to Catherine. I didn't want to share the journals with investigating eyes. I didn't want them to live outside their safe cave in Mrs. Judson's tidy kitchen. I didn't know really what I would be giving anyone, Brooke, Chuck or the police, and I may not have time to read more in them before I had to turn them over.

I could lie to the police, I believed in my ability to do that, to tell them I remembered Catherine telling me about Robert's warning, etc., but my poker face was limited to inquiry of patients, not investigative probing by people who knew how. I remembered Brooke's admonition that I was not as smart as I thought I was. No one had ever said that to me before, but I knew she was right. And I was pretty certain I couldn't lie to her, and I didn't want to be so blatantly dishonest with Chuck.

A car honked behind me, and I realized the left-turn arrow was green. I edged my car onto Cantrell, and as I coasted and braked down the winding hill, I knew I was not ready for what would happen if I told the detectives or anyone about Robert. I wouldn't be able to control the knowledge once it left my mouth. I still felt desperate to know what he knew, what he wasn't telling me. I needed more information. Then I could make a better decision about what to share with the police, or if it were all a red herring and Robert could be left out of the investigation completely. And even if I knew what he did about these men Tyler was hanging around with, what did Catherine have to do with them?

Sitting at the light on Cedar Hill, I tried to come up with some way I could make the connection between those men and Catherine without inviting inquiry into her relationship with Robert, but none of them seemed like a story I could manipulate once I told it. And the second I connected her with that family, even though they worked together, the detectives would assume an affair. There was always an affair in police dramas on TV.

And, of course, if they caught me in one lie, they might return to me as a suspect. Then I'd never be able to find her and get her back.

The light changed and I continued on Cantrell through Riverdale toward the next light by the Exxon, flipping the narrative and thinking about how much I would enjoy the trouble Robert would get into for being involved with a subordinate at a state agency, especially given the prominence of his new position. He would probably lose his new job because his affair with Catherine wasn't just immoral — from what I understood, it was illegal. He had approved some of her release time and special projects she was given as an assistant professor. However, punishing him like that would mean humiliating Catherine publicly at a time when all I wanted was to have her back, to really get her back, all the way back. Forgiven back.

And I would be humiliated, too. I would forever be linked with Robert, any time my name was mentioned. It could mean career suicide. For both of us.

I crossed the intersection and moved into the left-turn lane to drive into the gas station parking lot, to turn around and go home. I was not ready to talk to the police, to unleash all this on him, on me, on Catherine. I could get there, I thought. I could be ready. I knew Chuck could help me, and even Brooke would have advice about what to do.

But as I thought these things, I could feel that deep mental current stirring below, moving in the opposite direction, and I knew I couldn't, I didn't want to, withstand that undertow.

I pulled to a stop parallel with Cantrell and sat with my foot on the brake, trying to clear my mind to make the decision of whether to drive home through Riverdale, by the Big Dam Bridge and the running path, or to return the way I had come via Cantrell Road and the Heights. The sun was bright on the concrete road and through the denuded trees, but my car felt dark, in shadows.

I scanned the parking lot while weighing my options and immediately tensed when I saw Robert two cars ahead of me. He finished with the pump, replaced the nozzle in the station tank, screwed on his gas cap, shut the tank cover and strode inside the Exxon. He hadn't seemed to see me or be conscious of being watched. I slipped a little lower in my seat, backed up to the edge of the parking lot from where I could more easily escape onto the road whichever way he went and waited for him to come out. I felt unfinished with him, both attracted and repelled.

In a few minutes, he stepped outside through the dirty, tinted glass doors, holding a bottle of water and his phone. As he moved toward his car, he answered his cell, and when he did his posture shifted. Where he had been forceful, tall, commanding, he now stooped slightly, and scanned the street and the parking lots. I dropped down lower and watched him skulk to his car.

He accelerated out of the lot going west on Cantrell, where he zipped in his powerful car into the left-hand traffic lane. I followed him.

When the light turned green, we moved straight ahead. I followed one car back or immediately behind in the other lane. I knew he might see me, but I was too scared to lose him. My hands shook. For the first time in my life, I felt like I might be in real danger. But as soon as he passed the Kavanaugh intersection, entering the old-money section of the city where even the homes on this busy thoroughfare were mannered and impressive, I knew Robert wasn't going home or back to work.

I probably wouldn't have followed him at all if I hadn't seen the change in him when he took that call. He reinforced my suspicions when he looked around and seemed to sneak to his car, his body language loudly and violently asserting that he was submitting to the person on the phone while also trying to pretend to have some control. He could never not see himself as in control. It must have killed him that Catherine ended the affair, that she made a decision, and he didn't get to make any, and then to go home to his wife, righteous in her wounds. Now someone else seemed to be controlling him, too.

After we crossed Kavanaugh and continued west on Cantrell, past the "Gucci" Kroger, toward University, I began to notice another car following Robert — or me — making a trio of vehicles moving amoeba-like along the four- and sometimes five-lane road. I switched to the right lane, as Robert was still in the left-hand traffic lane, and hung back as much as I dared to see if it was him or me the other driver was interested in, and then chastised myself for the assumption that because I was following Robert, any car going in the same direction at the same time must be following him or me as well.

I stopped self-flagellating when I saw Robert angle into the left-turn lane at University and the third car do the same, keeping a car between them. They were yielding to oncoming traffic, waiting to turn, and I was able to maneuver behind the third car, a black Lexus crossover vehicle — an RX350, the polished model number shone on the back hatch. Robert turned, and the car behind him did as well, but then oncoming traffic prevented the Lexus and me from following him when the light turned yellow and then red. I watched as Robert, going south on University, disappeared from view, but I believed the Lexus would take me to him.

As I waited for the light, I felt a cold grip of caution, or fear, in my stomach. I felt out of control — and when I began to inventory everything I'd taken and imbibed in the past few days, I knew I shouldn't be driving. This was ridiculous on the surface, but as soon as I had seen that other car, something caught me; there was something gripping me, something existed outside of me, of my car, of my mind and of my suspicions and assumptions, something that connected me to Catherine.

"This is not smart," I said aloud to myself. "This is not smart. Not smart, not smart." I wished I had Lavinia with me to talk to, to protect me, to protect. The sense of danger was in the air, omnipresent, inescapable. I couldn't free myself and drive home now. I was being towed forward by the Lexus.

When the left-turn arrow flashed, I followed the car around the corner and south on University. I couldn't see Robert's car in traffic ahead of us, and I scanned the parking lots along University and the side streets to see if he had been waiting to catch the Lexus, but his silver Mercedes didn't appear.

"Shit-shit-shit-shit-shit." My chanting switched as I found that, distracted by the search for Robert, I wasn't behind the Lexus anymore. I searched in my rearview mirror for it, but there was more than one black vehicle in the lanes behind me, and I was unsure of what to do next. I pounded the steering wheel, and pulled toward the right lane. The fear still felt all around me, though. I still wasn't ready to drive home.

I turned off University at the mall, and pulled into the underground lot. I wanted somewhere quiet and dark to clear my head and think. I would act as my own therapist and "take this apart," as I often said to my clients who were making rash decisions based on likely false or incomplete assumptions.

I turned off the engine. My heart rate was elevated, my focus was blurred, and I was panting, almost as if I had been running. I could feel the sweat under my arms and the back of my neck under my sweater and jacket, that surplus warmth meeting the cold air seeping into the car right on my skin. I closed my eyes and tried to calm my breath. My thoughts were helter-skelter: between the bizarre thoughts that I needed to get back on the treadmill regularly, I could see the Lexus again, and realized I knew the last three letters of its Arkansas license plate, HZE. I tried again to slow my breathing and let my thoughts flow to see if I could remember the first three numbers, but nothing came, and I feared I would make something up to fill in the gap if I kept trying to force it.

Again, I tried to slow my breath and began to count inhalations. By the time I got to 10, I felt more in control, my heart wasn't racing in my chest to distraction, and I could focus on counting instead of feeling barraged by images and fleeting thoughts. I opened my eyes.

Parked nose to nose with my car in the mall ramp was the black Lexus RX350. I recognized the two men as those from the following and tailing dodge-and-weave on Cantrell. One polished looking, or at least as if he could be driving the Lexus, the other more like the men Catherine described in her journal, "...*not office or politico types you find around these bank towers near the Capitol in LR.*" Not someone who could easily fit into a corporate office or a lobbyist role, rumpled, a little tough. Pale. Thin. Haggard. I saw the word written in my mind as soon as I thought it: Meth.

I met the gaze of the driver, kitty-corner across from me, who was sitting, unencumbered by a seat belt. His door was slightly ajar, and the overhead light of the car was on. The passenger also wasn't wearing a seat belt. They were both watching me. None of us moved, and then I jerked automatically when my phone began to vibrate with a call. Without moving my head, I dropped my gaze down to the screen and saw it was Chuck. I was tempted to answer it and see if I could somehow get him to stay on the line, but I rejected the call.

"Meth" got out of his side of the car and stood by the door, and then the passenger must have also exited because he was standing suddenly at my passenger door. I unlocked the car, and Meth got in beside me, while the slick man sat cross-ways behind me, so I could see him in the rear-view mirror, acting as if I was picking him up, as if we knew each other well. Had the door opened and shut? I hadn't heard it or felt its thud. His colleague looked ahead, but he didn't seem high. He seemed very aware, twitching in the direction of the slightest sound, such as the creaking of the other man's leather jacket, directly behind him.

"You are Mr. Catherine?" "Meth" asked upon shutting the door and flicking the locks.

"That's what we've been calling you," the man in the back seat said. His English carried a vague accent, slightly purer vowels, fewer consonants given short-shrift, as if he had come to America at age eight or nine, just past the cognitive cut-off for assimilating another language as naturally as the first. Something from his past seemed to hang on him. He looked directly at me in the mirror. He was slight, too, but not in an unhealthy way, with dark sculpted, thick hair that would have been curly if it had been allowed to be. As it was, it looked nearly like cement. He had clear green eyes, like jade. He did not look at me.

"I am," I confirmed. I was about to ask about her, if she was okay, if she was alive, but I was afraid, of both the answers and of this cold, controlled man, who looked like he was around my own age, yet unnaturally preserved. He made no unnecessary movements. He kept looking straight ahead, right into my gaze whenever I raised my eyes, with his eyebrows elevated slightly, as if he were expecting something or as if he were about to take a deep breath...

I was wary of Meth in a different way, a way I had learned to fear people with nothing to lose, who had profited from cruelty and evil, had gotten ahead after the moral sunk costs of their initial crimes had been paid.

"I didn't expect to see you today," he said, almost purring. I regretted leaving my house, starting this whole chain of events, feeling as if I were running full speed at a wall, and I couldn't veer, couldn't stop. He could feel my thin reins of control slipping.

Meth turned toward me then, and I leaned back and away into my door. He didn't actually smell bad, but he looked so rough, so unwashed, that I was repulsed. It felt like touching him would be the end of something in me.

"I knew we would end up talking to you," he said. His voice was hoarse, but still very youthful, as if he hadn't quite grown up into a man's body.

"About Catherine?"

"Robert isn't as savvy as he wants to be, I think. Do you think that?" I saw the mouth moving of the man in the back seat. He looked me in the eyes, and this time I met his gaze, though it turned my stomach.

I said nothing.

He looked at me for a second or two. Meth turned forward and gazed without interest into the mostly empty garage.

Then he said with control that chilled me even more, "So here is what you're going to do."

Almost talking over him, the man behind me said: "I think that Robert is not savvy. If he were savvy, he could have kept all of this from happening. Now you will have to be savvy to have any hope that you can save her, and maybe you can have a little revenge in the end, as well."

• • •

This is when I first began to fear that Catherine wouldn't come home. I had been acting on the idea that she would return to me, and that protecting her reputation and keeping myself out of the police station would contribute to that, but now, after seeing these men, my worry changed to dread, darkening everything around me, and the future I tried to look into.

And I knew that whatever happened to her, Robert was to blame.

With some of the power I had had over my thoughts when I suspected Catherine to be having an affair, I flattened this darkness, tried to put it down below my hopes for her safe return, but these mental muscles were overused and weakened, and despite acting as if I believed the accumulating lies, I was afraid to face what was moving from unthinkable to possible: I would never see her again. And yet, I acknowledged, Robert had given me a little hope because he knew, or thought he knew, who was a threat to her or who might have her now. Still, the waves of doom were washing up within me. I couldn't shake them.

• • •

When I am honest with myself, I know that I don't really remember what this icy man looked like very clearly, though I saw him more in the days to come. I've created this image, this memory in my mind, down to his seemingly brand-new black leather jacket, the black leather gloves he held in one of his hands, his black cashmere sweater, his pale skin, his searing eyes, his silken, vaguely but unrecognizably accented English, because this is how he must have looked to provoke the reactions I had to him: repulsion, a visceral aversion on a nearly cellular level, and yet a desire to submit, and, sometimes, even to please him.

And the tormenting faint scent of Shalimar lingers with these memories, as well.

I never described him to anyone else, never wrote down any details of his appearance at the time, and of course have no photos and did not know his real name. He called himself "D."

"Where are you from?" I asked him, sitting there, afraid not only to take my eyes off Meth, sitting next to me, jerking and nervous, but also to look at him.

"I, like you, I am trying to resolve...all this."

Against the deeper, dreadful knowledge, I felt a small surge of hope. I needed to. I tried to control myself, but I felt ridiculous with both of them.

"Please— I..." I couldn't finish the sentence. I saw I didn't need to.

"This isn't social hour," said Meth. "I know what you want, of course. You want your wife back."

"You, I'm sure, you love your wife," said D. He glossed over the word "love" strangely. Was it an accusation? Was it sarcasm? Irony? A euphemism? I said nothing, knowing I had no power, no control of the situation. "You want her back."

"Yes."

"I want to give her back. I don't like this kidnapping shit," said Meth.

"That would be nice, ideal, even," came from behind me.

"You haven't told the police, right? About Robert?" said Meth. It was as if they were two voices for one side of a conversation, two very different voices. I shook my head.

D spoke again. "This is a good thing. This is good, because we can leave it among all of us, where it should be left. Do you agree this is best?"

I have a memory of him smoking then, slowly pulling on the cigarette, even more slowly exhaling the smoke, and yet it doesn't seem possible. The next time I was in my car, I smelled no cigarette smoke, only Catherine's Shalimar.

"I want my wife back."

"That is agreement, then? Yes, yes, I can see that it is. Robert is not so agreeable, because Robert confuses himself with those who have control of this situation. That is how this situation, well...arose."

Meth was watching me stare into the rearview mirror and laughed. "Are you worried about being followed?"

He looked at something toward the mall entrance.

"Don't mind him; it is too late for him," D said in a lower, more silken voice, inclining his head toward Meth.

"It is probably too late for Robert," Meth answered, almost on top of D, ignoring him. "It could be too late for Catherine, but it is not too late for you, not at all. Not yet."

He put his hand on the handle, but didn't open the door. I did not know what to ask or say in response. My internal organs had all been frozen by his casual threat to Catherine — or to the hope I had for her. But I was afraid they would leave without telling me what I could do to save my wife.

"What is the next step?" I was falling back on my therapy training, because I couldn't think of anything else to say.

"The next thing to do is not to do anything with the police. Don't be some kind of hero." said Meth. "And say nothing to that lawyer who was on the news. That blonde."

I nodded.

"I think you will cooperate because, of your own accord, you have not done this already," elaborated D.

Meth opened his door, staying aware, still jumpy, even. His adrenaline seemed high, while D was calm, centered.

"You're not loaded, right? But you have influence," Meth said.

"I don't have millions of dollars hidden away, but if you want money for Catherine, some kind of ransom, I can get it. I can get *thousands,* but it will take several days, maybe, well..."

D chuckled behind me.

"No one is interested in your 401(k)." Again, I was somehow unsurprised by his ability to guess what I would propose, just repulsed by it. "But my friend is interested in what you can do."

"Could you save Catherine? Let me find her? Bring her home?" I asked them both.

"He could, yes. He could," said D.

Meth turned. "We want actual money, real money. What Tyler owed us—" he didn't stop to explain — "and what do you call it? Hardship pay. We want hardship pay, and I think you can help get it."

"I have about $25,000 in an account I could get tomorrow." I was already starting to think about how quickly I could get the money Catherine and I had been saving to make a down payment on a lake house about an hour from Little Rock, which had doubled when she got her new job's signing bonus. I didn't know how I could get it — I'd already thought through all of the monetary possibilities when she disappeared, hoping for a ransom request.

They both smiled, and Meth rolled his eyes. Then D's expression returned to glass, and he didn't move or shift in his seat.

"I'm not against you, 'Mr. Catherine,' and I am certainly not against your lovely wife, who is of everyone most certainly the biggest victim of all this." Again, I felt the chill at the core of me when he spoke of Catherine, more when he seemed to be trying to show compassion toward her — or was it a blanket accusation of the rest of us? What had I done? Wasn't I innocent?

He nodded his head toward Meth, who got out of the car and shut his door, and then turned and opened D's. He leaned in across D. I again felt the sweat on my neck and under my arms, and as I heard Meth moving slowly toward me from the back seat, I felt a cold point of pressure on the back of my neck. I closed my eyes.

"Okay," Meth directed. He was more focused than I had seen him. "You are not the money; you are the way to the money. And when you get the money we want from the person we want it from, then we'll all have what we want."

"What happens with Catherine?" I asked. I whispered it; I hated saying her name around them.

He ignored me, and I wasn't sure if I had said it aloud.

"You're going to get Robert to give us his fucking money so we can be done with this whole fucking mess."

"Robert? What do you mean?"

"Tyler tried to get real money from him. I mean real money, like, I guess, millions?" He seemed to be asking me, as if I would know. I shrugged. "But he wouldn't really go for it himself. Really, he wanted *us* to do all the work, take all the risk."

"Tyler? Tyler Gewinn you're talking about, right?"

"Yeah, I know him from high school. He used to hang around with Keller. The whole thing was his idea; he's the one who told me and Justin about the affair your wife and his dad had." He looked up at me like he might be about to say something about blurting something like that out, querying, even a little shy looking, and he looked then, very young, just a kid, a horrifying child, and then he shrugged off any discomfort he might have felt. I blinked quickly, but kept watching him. He was still twitchy, but the cold point of pressure remained in place.

"Could you, I'm sorry, could you tell me your name, or a name to use for you?"

He said his name was Ryan and didn't mention a last name.

D moved over as Ryan started to sit down practically on top of him in the back seat and the cool weight on my neck was gone. I saw the shadow of the gun in my rearview mirror as Ryan returned it to its hiding place on his body. I'd thought Ryan was the flunky, but now I was unsure.

"He owed Justin some money, and then, me, too, so when we started to get more serious about getting it, he was all, 'Man, I'm unemployed. I don't got it,' and on and on. But Justin's mean about money, and he really does this shit more than me. He wasn't giving up. He told Tyler to figure something out, and that's when Tyler said we could get the money and lots more to divide up from his dad if we bribed him."

"Bribed? Why were you bribing him?"

He looked at me, uncomprehending and angry.

"Do you mean 'blackmailed'?" I asked.

"Yeah, shit, I always mix those words up. Yeah, *blackmailed*." He was such a novice criminal, he didn't even have the vocabulary to describe his actions — or the sense to stop telling me everything he and his gang were trying to do. "So we went to Robert and we told him we would tell people about the messing around, and he would lose his fancy-ass, big-money job and probably get in real shit for his old job where he was — cuz of his affair, but he just fucking said no, he wouldn't pay. He said nothing happened, he wasn't going to pay because he was innocent, and even if he wasn't, if he just paid us, we'd always be coming back for more. He didn't take it serious at all."

"He said this to you and to Tyler?" I had the feeling Ryan was rarely asked questions, and he was enjoying this moment of being in charge.

"No, to me and Justin. He didn't know Tyler was behind it, but really, the whole thing started because Tyler owed the money. That's when Keller got really pissed and decided that we needed a lot more money, not just what Tyler owed, and this guy could pay it, and he wanted Tyler to go and get it, stop hiding behind us — we'd just done it that way because Tyler told us he was more likely to pay it to keep Tyler out of it."

He took a breath and studied the back of his left hand, where there were three half-inch scratches.

"We told Tyler that he should go back and ask for the money, the real money we were pretty sure we could get, but Tyler wouldn't do it. Justin figured out that now that we had the idea, we didn't need Tyler, and we did *not* need to be fucking around with that shit — someone who wouldn't pay, had big ideas, wouldn't do any of the work. No one really needed Tyler. He was a dick.

"Little fucker owed money, not just to us, and not just for drugs and shit either. Degenerate was a fucking gambler, too. Those guys like Keller don't mess around. We did him a favor, made him a sad little victim with the way he died. Those other guys would have made it pretty clear how worthless he was."

The casual excitement in his voice chilled me. I looked down at my own hands, and when I looked up, they were both standing outside the car, with D looking down at Ryan in bemusement, as if he were watching the village idiot unwittingly dig his own grave.

"I don't know what to do next," I called out to them. They turned toward me simultaneously, mirror images of movement, opposites of persona and demeanor.

"Think it over. I'll be in touch — or Keller will. Now you know who we are and what you're going to do. ... And what you're not going to do, right?"

I nodded.

As Ryan walked back to the driver's side opposite me after shutting my car's rear door, D turned and mouthed something. I wasn't sure what, but it seemed like he was saying, "Make Robert pay."

They got in their Lexus, and before I had time to put my key in the ignition, their car had backed out of the parking space ahead of me and disappeared.

• • •

I sat on the deck in my winter coat, hat and gloves for about 20 minutes when I got home, before I let out the dogs. I needed time to sort through everything, but my mind was blank; every time I would start to concentrate on some detail or try to plan what I needed to do next, I lost the thought, and my mind was filled with a hard, bright void. Minutes later I would realize I was staring at the leafless trees, having made no plan and gained no understanding.

The distance was growing between the surface thoughts of reporting all of this to the police and the undertow of secrecy. There was a middle ground, to tell Brooke. Maybe she would know what to do. I owed her a phone call I was procrastinating returning. I didn't want to go into her office, meet, talk to her at all. But I knew it was possible the police might be watching me, or at least aware of where I was going and who I was talking to. They still did not seem to suspect me, but Brooke's words continued to echo: "You don't know what they know. You are not as smart as you think you are."

I knew it was dangerous, but this is when I started to believe I was more capable of bringing Catherine home on my own. If there was any chance of getting her, I needed to do what Ryan and D said. I needed to keep the secret. I went inside to let the dogs out. And I would keep my own secrets, for just a little longer.

I suppose I felt the same kind of hubris that must have powered Catherine's affair. I never thought she wanted to hurt me. Whatever she wanted — distraction, validation, sex with someone new? — she believed she could get away with, until she made a decision, or one was made for her, such as by Tyler, with Robert as his proxy. She didn't know how well I observed her, how her little poker player-like tells, her obsession with her phone, her longer hours, her distraction and moodiness when she was with me, broadcast her crime. She wasn't as good a liar as she thought she was. How good was I at hiding all of this? All of that?

Surprising myself, I picked up the phone and pressed Brooke's name in my contacts. It felt with just that motion I was relieving myself of a huge burden. It must have been her cell, as she answered herself, abruptly, casually.

"Brooke?"

"Yes, how are you doing?"

"I thought I'd check in...?" Now that I heard her cold, unwelcoming voice, I was losing my nerve.

"Yeah, something's going on with the investigation, and they aren't talking to me — or to Chuck, which is weird. I thought it was bad news for you, maybe, but nothing actually points to that, no warrants, the stuff they took from your house hasn't been examined."

"How do you know that?"

"We know what goes on with investigations. The police are a public entity, and when they're doing things, procedural acts go along with them and we aren't seeing any of that. It's like, you know, bubbles on the surface of a pond when something is happening below the surface. So, they are off you, at least for now."

"Do you know who they're on to?"

"That I cannot tell, but I may know in a couple of days...I know that seems like forever when you're waiting for news of Catherine, but I think we'll get there sooner than we think."

I wavered. I opened my mouth to tell her about D and Ryan, about Robert and Catherine, but she interrupted me.

"She is such a wonderful woman. I just know she'll be okay," she said. The sincerity and warmth were unusual, the focus and edge were gone.

"You know her?"

"I knew her," she said. "I don't mean — please — I don't mean that she's gone," she said, catching herself quickly. "I mean I used to know her. We were friends in high school and stayed in some touch after. We were pretty close when I was in law school and she was getting her MBA."

I did some calculating on the timing. "You were friends when I met her?"

"Oh, you didn't know that? I'm *how* you met her. I brought her to Chuck's party, the party where you first talked to her. She never told you that?"

"No...you and Chuck were..."

"Yes, she probably told you about that."

"No, she never did. Honestly, I'm sorry, I don't think I'd heard your name before Chuck referred me to you."

"Hmm," she mused, breathily, a voiced sigh. "Wow. That surprises me."

"Why is that? Were you that close?"

"No, it surprises me because she ended our friendship over my affair with Chuck. I was married, so was he, and she was really offended by it. It wasn't dramatic, just a slow easing away from me. By the time things ended between me and Chuck, as they were always going to do, she and I weren't in touch anymore, so I never told her about it, never got to tell her she'd been right."

"But—" It almost came out then, I nearly revealed Catherine's hypocrisy to her former friend, but there was almost a physical barrier between me and this kind of disloyalty to my wife, though the urge to commiserate was strong.

"It's okay. We all do the best we can," she said. "I missed her, but I understood. If you do shit like that, you have to take the consequences, and they may not come from those you expect."

I was silent, until she asked me if there was anything else. We hung up.

And so I hadn't told. That meant I had to wait until told what to do, but this made me more afraid of the police than the men in the car, because if they figured out what I was doing, if they interfered, it wouldn't matter if I had told them; the outcome for Catherine would be the same. As I thought about what had to happen next in order to do what this strange gang had ordered, I had trouble imagining her back at home with me and the dogs. I could not envision her, after all of this, sitting calmly, quietly, in our kitchen with Lavinia curled up on the floor around her chair legs. I could not conjure any image of her in our home, even wounded, beaten, a victim. When I thought of her, I was picturing her almost exclusively from the years before she had the affair, sitting reading or working on her laptop, nursing a cup of coffee, maybe for hours, drinking it cold, noticing me, smiling up at me, saying nothing, taking a fraction of her attention and dividing its intensity to give me some of it, to acknowledge me and see me, and to take a small, passing, meaningless moment, and to fill it with the two of us, and the meaning of what we were together.

A smile might do it, perhaps, or I might look up to find her merely watching me as I read, puttered or pet the dogs. Her gaze was soft, with crinkles around her eyes, not from smiling, but from focusing — on me. I wasn't only grieving Catherine's absence these past few days, but also the ruination of what I believed our marriage to be, a grief that was more than a year old. And I knew I would have to grieve all the lost opportunities of the twelve months in between when I could have accepted her as she was and loved her expansively enough to encompass not just her flaws, but her needs, instead of loving her so narrowly as to blind myself to them and her. She was, she *is,* a broken woman with this painful capacity for secrecy who wanted not to be secretive, but to be known and seen and loved, as she knew and saw and loved me, hoping to return to something from before, but incorporating the losses and betrayals into a new life that wove them into its daily moments along with the reassurances of love and acceptance. Perhaps that is what I was unable to envision, not the return of the criminals' hostage, but a return of a Catherine I had stopped seeing some time ago, and, honestly, a Catherine I had never seen in some ways. I was desperate to really know her, for that clear and open image to emerge.

And before I could wallow in this image any more, the strange dream-like moment came back to me from the day before, this distant and misty Catherine, sitting right next to me, uncomprehending, unreachable.

• • •

I wanted nothing more than to hibernate — I had canceled all my patient appointments until further notice — but Chuck rang my doorbell around 4 p.m. The sound of the bell startled me, frightened that it might be Ryan or D, but even as I thought it, I knew they wouldn't come to my house in daylight, so easily observed — and D wouldn't ring the bell. I felt raw and wary when I saw him, as I'd been drinking, of course, but I still had the presence of mind to know I might make a drunken confession I'd regret.

I was ready for the impulse to confide all in Chuck, to unburden myself to my friend. I knew he was trustworthy, a safe psychological harbor. He had talked to me at length over the years about how similar our professions were, our oaths of confidentiality that were so internalized. He knew things about my friends and neighbors that they wouldn't even confess to me, a therapist, partly because he could be trusted in a kind of legal, official way, but mostly because he could protect them, and there was strength behind Chuck's promise. All I did was nurture and support. He fought. He advocated. He defended. If I confessed all to him — Catherine's affair, my dealings with these shadowy figures, their expectations of me — he would fight and advocate for me. He would defend me. I wouldn't have to pay him; it was his nature.

But I couldn't bring myself to do it, and as he sat in the living room that night, nursing his scotch, while I sipped my own after finishing off a pot of coffee, I knew I would not tell him about Catherine's infidelity.

"It is so strange to be here without her around, checking my drink—"

"And your coaster," I answered, handing him one.

I was conscious of a shifting in the dynamic of our friendship. I wondered if he was, too. We'd known each other since our undergraduate years, before he went to law school at U of A and I went to get a counseling degree there. He knew my first wife, and about those problems, which were about personalities, not infidelities. I was a year younger than he was, but I had always played the mature, thinking adult, even though in some ways, I followed him — to social groups, to friends, back to Fayetteville for grad school. Like all grad school experiences, there were wild times, fueled by ill-advised decisions. My own family had an alcoholic history, so I rejected many of these activities in favor of advancing my standing with the professors, with the psychological community, but Chuck engaged, had fun, wasn't hurt and lived to tell. Part of the reason he did was because of the times I helped him, lending him money, even keeping him from being arrested one night when drugs were found at a party the police raided. But through the years, I also saw that he didn't emerge unscathed from things; he just accepted the scars along with the consequences, and moved on. We both returned from Fayetteville to Little Rock after graduate school, married, I to my first wife, he to his first of four, so far, wives, and we maintained this dynamic. Why would it change? Even though he was an attorney, advising people all day, he asked me for advice, and I advised. I was cautious as we grew older: I looked for signals that he resented it and had grown past that, but I never saw any.

But tonight, I felt this shift. He had talked me into retaining Brooke, and I had done what he said. This was an area I knew nothing about, but he lived in it. He knew the players and the patterns. I felt the sting of having to accept his wisdom. And after all this time, I saw that maybe he did resent me a little, or at least was cognizant enough of this dynamic not to tell me everything, not of his affair with Brooke, or even that Brooke had been friends with Catherine.

"I have to tell you something, Chuck," I said, picking up my scotch and swirling the glass to watch the alcohol's legs grow on the crystal and then dissipate.

"Yeah?"

"Today, I started to feel like she's not coming home."

"You can't think like that, man. I mean, you gotta focus on doing everything you can to get her back."

He had no idea how much I was doing.

"No, I mean, I wouldn't act on it. I guess it's just fear, manifesting as some kind of internal prophecy."

"Oh, are we gonna get Baptist now? Pentecostal, I mean?"

"Not that kind of prophecy. No, I mean those moments when your apprehensions about the future feel like fact."

"As in...?"

"Well, you know everyone thought Sandra left me kind of suddenly?"

"We had just been to Heber with you! Everything seemed fine!" he said, remembering our weekend at the lake in which our routine cordiality helped our friends think that we were a happy couple, that we would endure.

"It was and wasn't sudden for her."

"Meaning?"

"We weren't that compatible — I've told you this, not just in our daily habits and routines, but in our approaches, in our values. I mean, etcetera, etcetera, it's that long boring story."

"You've never really told me." He leaned forward in his chair, cupping his scotch in his hands.

"We can talk about it someday, but that's not why I mention it. No, I was thinking about the fear-as-prophecy phenomenon."

"She had a fear of staying married to you?" he laughed.

"Yeah, actually, I think she did, one she wouldn't admit to herself."

He leaned back and looked down, a little embarrassed, I thought, when I noticed a little color in his cheeks.

"The truth was, or one of the truths was, she wanted children, and she wouldn't admit it to me because I didn't. She didn't want to fight with me, she just sublimated that desire until it became intolerable and manifested as prophecy."

"What do you mean, prophecy? That she'd die, childless, alone somewhere, eaten by her 90 cats, years after you had left this mortal coil?"

"No, no." I smiled. "She was at a meeting at the Little Rock Club, a professional society she sometimes attends. She told me she was standing at the windows, looking out at the view. You know how you can see the Capitol and the Arkansas River, and the city just lying there before you?"

He nodded.

"I didn't know it, but she'd had a really tough year, wrestling with this desire for children, with her commitment to our marriage, she felt very depleted and discouraged, resigned, really. And she told me, the day she said she was leaving me, that she had the strongest premonition of her life — the only time she'd felt like premonitions could exist, and could be true — that she would be dead a year later. That she wouldn't be back for that meeting the next year."

"What? Did she want to kill herself? That doesn't seem like Sandra. She's so can-do." I could see him reflecting on what he knew of her, trying to square this revelation with his experiences.

"No, not at all. Just a belief that something outside herself, beyond her control would kill her."

He waited.

"It was probably five months later that she told me she was going. She knew enough, as a psychiatrist, about how to dig down into those feelings, find their origins, and what she realized was that something in her was dying in our marriage, and if she were to stay, she would lose too much."

I had never talked to him like this about my divorce. He was leaning forward, but his face was directed down, studying the carpet, curious but cautious. The operator wanted more but was being careful not to push too hard.

"She had Miles so quickly after she married Dave," he said, thinking aloud. "I thought it was an accident."

"You should know better there!" I laughed. "Nothing with Sandra is accidental."

"Yeah, you're right. I know. She's a planner!" I could tell he was thinking about the only trip the four of us took together, beyond our Arkansas weekends, a road trip to Chicago. Sandra gave us itineraries every morning, with detailed schedules and suggested wardrobes.

"I'm trying not to believe the prophecy my fear is turning into," I confessed.

"Yeah," he said, downing the last of his scotch before I refilled his glass. "Good luck with that."

• • •

I didn't sleep very well again that night. I dozed, but it was probably more like passing out. I thought I heard Catherine in the other room with the dogs, but when I woke fully, they were on their beds in our room. I had gone out into the kitchen, sure I heard her making coffee, her little absentminded humming of "Long and Winding Road," that seemed to follow her wherever she went, which she would always deny when I asked her why that song, of all the tunes known to man.

Lying in the darkness, I watched the ceiling fan at the far end of the bedroom Catherine liked to turn on for white noise. I took something Sandra had brought me out of a sample box, but I didn't care enough anymore to read what it was. I tried to sort through everything I had learned and then began to worry about how Ryan would reach me, if it would invite renewed police scrutiny. Could they charge me for obstruction? Would my attorney abandon me for lying to her by omission? They had left no directions, no meeting point, no time. Maybe they didn't really know how to proceed. These thoughts badgered me from the corners of my mind, off and on, as I dozed in fits and restlessly lay in the dark room.

At 5 a.m., I gave up on sleep and got up to walk the dogs. Maybe Ryan would find me, or this mysterious Justin, wanting to get their plan in motion. I let Wesley and Lavinia out in the backyard while I got my winter walking clothes on, a layer of fleece and my heavier jacket, with heavy, old-fashioned sweatpants, Smartwo ol socks and trail-running shoes Catherine had given me. I was looking for my gloves in the car when I saw the paper in the driveway and went to retrieve it.

It was Sunday. I'd had no idea.

Day Six

6

SITTING WITH MY GLOVES and the paper at the kitchen table, waiting for the signal from the dogs that they were done in the yard, I paged through the paper and exhaled all the breath in my lungs when I saw a headline on the Arkansas section's front page, "LR man killed in apparent drug-deal fracas."

The identifying mug shot was Ryan. The last name listed was "Brendan." According to the story, he had been killed by several gunshots in Kanis Park just hours after I had left him with D.

> The police press release reports that two park-goers reported shots fired around noon as they got out of their cars at the recreation area. One person in the party phoned 9-1-1 to report the shots. Police responded to the call, and after a brief search discovered the body of a white male visible from the parking area a short distance into an overgrown section of the park. No one else was seen, and witnesses questioned at the park reported no other unusual activity.
>
> The victim is identified as Ryan Brendan, 24, in Little Rock. Police shared no details as to his occupation or family situation, but an investigation by newspaper staff indicates the victim has a record

of drug-related offences and arrests along with court-mandated rehabilitation for addiction and abuse of methamphetamines.

The man was dead when police located the body, apparently from two gunshot wounds to the head.

An investigation of the crime has been opened. Police are questioning known associates for information on Brendan's activities. An unnamed police source suggested that drug deals are often conducted in the area, and police are looking for frequenters of the park for questioning. The crime occurred outside the park's surveillance-camera range.

I dropped the paper. My hand was shaking. As I finally inhaled, I saw the dogs had been clawing at the back door and whining for at least a minute. In retrospect, their high-pitched barking whines had been the soundtrack for my reading. I rushed to let them in and then raced throughout the house to shut and lock every door and window, pulling each shade and blind and curtain. I was almost as afraid as I had been the morning Catherine disappeared.

At my desk, before 6 a.m., with the dogs sitting tense and alert, Lavinia by my feet, Wesley by the office door, I clutched my cellphone, turned it on, turned it off, turned it on, turned it off. The shock had momentarily sobered me, but I still could not think in straight lines. I really needed to call Brooke now, but I was so frightened of doing so, my shaking hands couldn't dial the numbers each time I made up my mind to go ahead. The adrenaline surge of the decision to report what I knew was stunted, abridged. My fear took over. I knew my actions of the last 24 hours or so would call more suspicion to me than to the real criminals, and if they found out...

Catherine's face in my memory of her of the other day, sitting with me on the deck started to blur and dissipate. I chastised myself aloud for the impulse to turn to the police. I wanted protection, but now was not the time to lose heart or endanger Catherine more than she already was. I hadn't even tried yet to get the money from Robert, to get Catherine released with the ransom they really wanted.

I remembered D's silken pronouncement that it was already too late for Ryan, and I thought of Robert, who had been next on his list of those in danger. I could only do what I'd been told to do, to get Robert to pay. To save Catherine.

I stood slowly, as straight and purposeful as I could. I snapped my fingers and said to Wesley's alert expression, "We're going for a ride." Both dogs scrambled up beside me, attentive but serious. They looked to me for what would happen next. I went to find my car keys, and they followed. I could hear their claws clicking on the wood floor through the otherwise empty house.

• • •

I parked outside of Robert's house on Crestview in Hillcrest. His car was in the driveway, and a second car, a Mercedes SUV, was parked directly in front of it in an open garage, which was alit. It was about 6:30 a.m. I didn't know what their Sunday routine might include, but I wanted to be here when he left the house. I turned off the car. The dogs sat looking at the window, following my gaze, watching his house, as well. Wesley was in the front seat next to me, Lavinia in the middle of the back seat, staring out between us. I wondered if they had been there before, with Catherine.

The large, two-story brick home, on what looked like a double lot, had a sunporch on the far side and living areas built over the attached garage as well. A privacy fence hid the back yard and much of the rear part of the house from street view. The uncurtained living room window revealed a faint glow of light from a room or hallway in the rear. Preparing for the day, I thought. Sitting, chatting over coffee.

I had nothing in the car except Lavinia to protect me, and if Robert were in danger, so was I, especially if I were anywhere in his proximity, but I couldn't sit in my house anymore, reading of and hearing about additional deaths, feeling they were coming for me and not being able to do anything to save Catherine, if anything could still be done. I'd end up reporting what I knew to someone, and everything would explode. Then anyone could be murdered — Chuck, Brooke, even Sandra.

"I hate him so fucking much," I said to Lavinia, who had moved so her front paws were on the armrest between me and Wesley, and her head was in line with mine, though slightly above me. She looked down into my face, and then back out the window. "But he is the only person who knows anything about this. I don't know what to do, and if they get him, too, I'll have to go to the police." As soon as I said that aloud, I wished I could take it back. I was overcome with the fear that just saying that in the car to my uncomprehending dogs was bait to a malevolent universe that seemed to be an accomplice to this cruel and violent gang of men, appearing from nowhere, a cloud of dangerous smog and smoke. Nothing felt more like a death warrant for Catherine and for myself than telling the detectives what had occurred in the past 24 hours.

Around 7:15, Robert emerged from a door into the garage and walked to his car. He was dressed for work — when wasn't he working — but he was alone. He seemed wary, scanning his yard, and then, when he got to the car, he turned and looked down the block toward the corner of Spruce, and back toward where I was parked. He looked into my car, parked alone on the street, immediately, and almost imperceptibly paused, then unlocked his car, put his briefcase on the driver's seat, shut the door, and then walked down the driveway toward me. He was purposeful, but unsure, lacking some of the confident rectitude I had become used to when he worked with Catherine. I kept looking around and watching the street up and down in front of his house as he drew closer to me and the dogs.

As he paused at the locked door, I ordered Wesley into the back. He jumped to wrestle with Lavinia, who made room for him, and then returned to her spot, her paws on the armrest, her head turned toward Robert as he sat in the passenger seat. I reached up to stroke Lavinia's head under her ear.

"So, you saw the story in the newspaper this morning?" Robert questioned. "And somehow you know who the dead kid is?"

I nodded but said nothing.

"Can I ask you what you know about him?" He was sitting as close to the door and as far from Lavinia as he could, which gave him about 8 inches between her muzzle and his head.

"I got exact directions from him yesterday on how to get Catherine back."

"Catherine's dead! Jesus Christ!" He spat the words, as if he were whispering a scream. "She's as dead as Tyler, and as dead as that worthless little meth-head was doomed to be all along. How can you be so fucking smart and such an idiot at the same time?"

I stared straight ahead, my mouth in a horrified, agape shape, but nothing came out. His bald assertion shocked me, and I felt a nauseating rage that had been percolating since I arrived in his neighborhood and saw his house.

He said with slightly more control, "She was dead months ago. We're all dead. We're just walking around until they knock us down."

I pushed down the impulse to yell at him, as well as a different, smaller voice that I refused to listen to. "I still don't get why they grabbed her if their problem was with you. I know — I know—" I put my hand up to keep him from reminding me of their connection. "But you weren't together anymore, were you? Why is she paying for Tyler's mistakes? She doesn't have money. You're the one with the money." I gestured to his house and his expensive cars.

"Honestly," he said and paused, this time clearly trying to decide what to tell me and just how honest to be. "I don't think they planned to involve her early on, but to them, everyone they know, or know of, exists for their use. Friend's got a business? Run drugs through it or launder money there. Cousin's got a liquor license? Use it to buy alcohol for your bar that doesn't. Those people are pathological liars, so I can't really tell, still, what's going on, what happened when, what's going to happen next. Don't fool yourself that you can, either."

I started to say something about the pot and the kettle, but he sighed and said quietly, looking out into the street toward his house. "If I could change anything in time, I would keep Tyler away from Justin, I would go back and keep him from meeting him. The addictions, the gambling, all that, I can handle that, but I can't handle pure evil."

I watched him, waiting for him to speak, finally, the truth. The dogs seemed to be listening to his every word as well.

"They knew from Tyler about her, and they knew she was a vulnerability for me, and that I — well, Petra — has money. They knew her first name, and they were trying to get me to take the bait, to succumb to their blackmail scheme, and they were getting frustrated.

You have to understand that it was very tempting to me, to pay them what they asked, an amount that would hurt us but not cripple us. It felt like a new life could finally open up for him, and for all of us." He looked again at the house.

"Did Petra know about this?"

"Of course, she did. I manage her family's money; I don't control it. She knew who all these hoods were and how they affected Tyler. I was very near to saying yes, but she said not to do it — and I agreed — because if we paid them, nothing could stop them from coming back, endangering him all over again and ruining us on every level, our family, financially, reputation, everything. She was adamant, and I supported her. She was right."

"She's not missing, though, is she?" I said, a bitter tone in my voice, masking the jealousy I felt for him that his wife was there, somewhere in that house. He still knew where she was, could touch and talk to her.

"Maybe not physically, but you try to live with that decision as a mother of a dead son, a son you blame yourself for not saving when you had a chance. Don't idealize our situation," he scoffed.

"Then when Tyler died, they came after me even more — more often, more desperately. The blackmail was still a possibility, of course; I was just as vulnerable. I think they could see that threatening more members of my family might push me too far, though I'm not sure what they thought I'd do differently...report them maybe? I don't know, but they knew who Catherine was, as I said, and she was just another person who was useful in some way to them, someone they could capitalize on, so they threatened me with more than blackmail. They said they would hurt her. They were trying to move this all forward in whatever way they could. Tyler owed them some money; I knew that. And I would have paid his debts, but now they wanted one million dollars. I was sure if I paid it, I would never be free of them.

"We'd lost our son, and we weren't particularly inclined to take action when it could no longer save him."

"Did Petra know about that?"

"No." He did not seem to be ready to elaborate.

"I think they were following me, then, trying to find her. They didn't know where she worked now. Tyler was dead, so they didn't know enough about her to be efficient about it, and I hoped they would give up. I told them repeatedly that I would pay what Tyler owed, but it needed to be in some form of a business deal, some partnership in that bar Justin's cousin owns, something like that, so there could be a contract or paper trail to protect us all, but Justin wasn't satisfied. He wouldn't back off, and he kept pushing for me, like he wanted me to say no so he could just keep coming at me."

"How did they find her?" I asked. Despite my best efforts, and my pulse beating loud in my ears, Robert was drawing me in to his story.

"I don't know. I didn't know they had until I saw the newspaper reports. And then, later that day, Justin came to me and asked for the money again and threatened her. I said I couldn't pay it, that it was tied up with Petra's family trust now after Tyler's death."

I became aware of someone screaming, deep and guttural, in the car. My hands, balled into fists, hurt and throbbed. Wesley was barking, low, and strong, in his warning way, and Lavinia, whose breath I could feel suddenly on my neck, was growling in an intense, controlled cadence. I stopped beating Robert's face, neck and his hands and arms, which he had thrown around to protect his head, as soon as I realized I was doing it, but not before I had bloodied his nose, ripped his shirt collar, and scraped his cheek with...what? My fingernails? My wedding band? He was protecting himself, but not fighting back.

As I sat back in the driver's seat, rubbing my aching hands, I could hear him panting heavily. We were both breathing hard.

"You're lucky I don't have a baseball bat." I wheezed. "You took her from me twice. Twice! You had an affair with her and shattered my marriage, and then you didn't tell her, you didn't even warn her that she was really in danger, and you didn't pay them when you could have, and now, she's... she's... She... might not come home." I couldn't say it, though a mental image of her coming home was harder to call up than ever. All I could see was that ghosted image of her on the deck, mouthing words to me, fading away.

I heard a strange choking sound and looked over to see that he was stooped in his seat, coat and scarf askew, shirt ripped, blood dripping down onto his tie and coat, hair mussed. It shocked me; his control was completely unmoored. His bent posture shook as he tried to pull himself together.

"Who killed Ryan?" He started shaking his head, and I thought he was gesturing that he didn't know, but he was trying to collect himself, shrugging his coat back into place, sitting up taller, searching for a handkerchief or Kleenex to wipe his face of sweat and blood. The sun was rising, and the pink light scattered all around us, but Robert was in the shadow of the car, gray and masked with darkness, still. I handed him a Starbucks napkin from the map holder in my door.

"Probably Justin, that little shithead. He killed Tyler, too, I'm sure. Fucker is mean. I mean, cruel."

"I thought maybe you killed him," I said, though I hadn't actually thought about it until that moment.

"I wish I would have," he stuttered, still distracted by his bleeding nose. "It would have felt great to end him. Shit. I can't go to this breakfast like this. I can't go in my house, either, not until Petra leaves for the airport. She's going to Europe with a friend," he said, answering me before I asked.

"Are you sending her there? To get her away?"

He shrugged. "I don't think I can get her far enough away to help her if they've decided they really want her dead, but maybe I'm overreacting. Maybe they are just a Little Rock gang. But at least two people are dead. And the only thing that might do any good for anyone is to be out of sight and out of mind. You're not helping yourself with your little stunt here today. They've probably seen all of this." He gestured to his face and bloody shirt. His composure was back.

I shook my head and felt a chill colder than the winter morning pervade the car.

He took a deep breath and started digging for his car keys. "I'm going to have to move my car until Petra leaves. I better do it sooner rather than later. She'll notice it if she hasn't already."

I unlocked the car doors, but he didn't move. A light came in the upstairs sunporch in his house, and he relaxed for a moment, receding more into the shadow. I didn't want him to leave too quickly; picturing myself with just the dogs in the car, I felt more isolated and alone than I had since I had started to suspect Catherine of cheating on me.

"If they contact you, do what they ask, and do what they tell you."

"From what I understand, that's not the strategy you followed," I said.

"So you should listen," he said without irony, getting out of the car and walking across the street and down the block to his car, brushing himself off as he went, trying to recover his stride and rearrange himself. I wondered as I started my own car if he would live to the end of the day. I hadn't the first idea what to do to make sure I did.

• • •

I had nowhere to go but home, but I drove back meanderingly, partly to watch for anyone following me, but more because I was reluctant to be cornered there. I had a fleeting image in my mind from a history book of Austrian royalty shooting the animals their paid beaters chased right up to the barrels of their guns. I felt like the prey, and maybe the beater, as well. I squeezed my eyes shut and then opened them wide, trying to concentrate on the road.

I noticed no one tailing me but felt hardly qualified to be certain. At home, I went up to take a shower. I stopped at the fridge to put some ice on my hand, which was really throbbing now. I took a Hydrocodone left over from a dental procedure Catherine had had last year, but I put my thumb over her name on the label as I popped the top and spilled out a pill. I put the newspaper with the story of Ryan's murder in the recycling, let the dogs out but called them back in quickly, and again went throughout the house checking the doors and windows. The sliders on the lower level were particularly concerning to me, and I double-checked all the latches, and then activated our alarm system throughout the house, retreating to our bedroom with the dogs, my laptop and cellphone to think.

If something happened to Robert, it would reverberate throughout the city and the state, certainly more than luckless "Meth" Ryan's death and also, probably, more than Catherine's disappearance. She was, I admitted to myself, a winsome victim — pretty, relatively young, the white, middle-class mystery *People* magazine and its readers loved to venerate. But Robert was a quasi-celebrity, a business and social lion, a possible political candidate, respected for his academic credentials and his "real-world" successes, friend of the governor and who knows who else, like the fictional main character of Jack Butler's *Living in Little Rock with Miss Little Rock*, which we'd all read when it came out. Arkansans now knew Catherine only as a victim, but Robert they already knew, if not as a friend, then as someone of influence they aspired to be, or against whom they nursed grudges and hoped for karma's response. If something happened to him, the investigation would be real and thorough, and, I was confident, it would come hard at me.

Lying on the bed in my flannel pajama pants and Razorbacks sweatshirt, legs spread out in front of me, computer on my lap, dogs on the bed and on the floor, I started to believe Robert that I would really never see Catherine again. I had already begun having difficulty envisioning it, but with Ryan and D I had let myself hope that I would be able to do something. I could save her. Only me.

Now I really feared she would disappear from my life, taking her body and her presence with her, as she had taken her attention all those months ago. In a sad way, it felt inevitable. She was gone before. Now she might really be gone.

• • •

I woke up several hours later, having actually slept, but feeling hungover from too much brandy and painkillers, and then I remembered my fury and dread. My head was pounding. I walked to the bathroom to urinate and maybe to shower, still trying to think through what was next. I was tempted to call Robert — perhaps because he was my only confidant now — but I was hesitant to use my cellphone for anything related to what had happened to Catherine.

It was not even noon. Ryan had said he would contact me. Would Justin know that? Would he come here? Would he contact me? Should I leave the house, hoping to see him? Or was that a sure way of inviting harm to myself? Justin seemed to be the one who had instigated the murder of Tyler, had probably orchestrated Catherine's kidnapping and had apparently killed Ryan. The word "mean" that both Ryan and Robert had used to describe him seemed to me to be an epic understatement. If I did what he said, would I be allowed to live? How could Catherine ever come home now?

I did not have the criteria to decide what to do. I kept trying to calm myself, breathe slowly, fixate on some factor that could help me make a decision. Making it easy for Justin to find me would make it possible for him, or for D, to kill me or have me killed. If I did go out, how could I protect myself? My visit to Robert had only paralyzed me more, even though I admitted to myself that I had hoped to get advice from him, even if indirectly. Like me, he was just trying to keep himself and his wife alive.

In the shower, I set the water at a temperature that was almost too hot to stand. I watched as my skin turned red and tried to take what I knew apart so I could plan a course of action. I couldn't stand just waiting here with the dogs, doing nothing to get what I most wanted: my wife. Clarifying that for myself, I decided to go out and look for Justin, hoping and simultaneously fearing that it would be D who would find me.

• • •

I decided to take Lavinia with me, and I left Wesley with the television on and a rawhide bone, a rare treat for him that occupied him completely, as we walked out of the house into the garage. Lavinia hopped into the passenger seat of my Subaru.

The only place I could think to go at 11 a.m. was the lower deck of the Park Plaza parking ramp, and I drove straight there, through our neighborhood to Indian Trail, through the wooded hills to Keightly, and across Cantrell where Mississippi began. I was driving down Mississippi to Markham when I noticed the black Lexus in my rearview. At first it was just hovering in my vision, but by the time I got near Park Plaza's surface lots, it was aggressively on my tail. I slowed to a crawl as a way of signaling I saw it, and as soon as I did, it passed me in the right lane, then merged immediately in front of me. I followed.

It turned north on University, continuing straight through the Cantrell intersection into the Heights residential neighborhoods north of the shops and restaurants on Kavanaugh. When I thought we were going to dead end at the Arkansas River bluffs, the Lexus turned left on Greenwood, traveling slowly for a couple of blocks, and then turning right on Sunset, across from a small park, and parked on the street in front of a spatial ranch home.

I pulled ahead to park, and before I got out of the car, I could see D and someone I assumed to be Justin get out of the Lexus and walk casually toward Baker Park, a small corner lot park I drove by often, but had never stopped in. It was another chilly January day, and the small play area was empty. "Everyone is at church," I thought, and quickly confirmed the day of the week in my mind; I was losing track. They moved in tandem toward the swings and sat down in two of them with one empty swing between them.

I approached, and D gestured that I should sit in the vacant seat. I felt the cold, flexible plastic seat through my jeans immediately. Without my gloves, the chains would have been too cold to hold. Reflexively, I pushed back, and began to sway back and forth. Justin joined me, but D's swing was still, moving only as if with the slight January breeze.

"Aren't you worried the cops will see you with me?"

"Worry about what I tell you to worry about," Justin answered, impatient.

"The police aren't watching you. We'd know." D soothed.

Like Ryan, Justin was in his 20s, but he did not look like he used too much of his own products. He wasn't corporate by any means in his worn brown cargo pants that looked like they might have cost more money than they were meant to look like they cost. He had on a gray sweatshirt, with black sleeves and a hood, and what looked like some kind of hunting vest over that as well as a brown knit stocking cap. He was thin, but looked fit and strong, dangerous. He reminded me of a lithe snake, or of a small shiny knife. His skin may have been naturally pale, but it was sun- and wind-worn. He looked at me, moving more and more slowly back and forth to his right, but didn't speak. He seemed impatient but gave the impression he was used to managing this attribute of his character.

D looked exactly the same, and though he was not in a warm car, but outside in the cold park, he appeared unfazed. Instead of looking like he was wearing his clothes, he seemed coated in them, as if he were inseparable from the dark leathers and heavy fabrics. Only his pale, narrow face was exposed.

"I didn't know what would happen, what was next, how you'd find me," I babbled.

"We can't really be seen at Catherine's house, of course," said Justin. "I just wanna get this going." It was the first time he'd spoken. His voice was raspy, and I couldn't tell if he had a cold or if he'd already smoked himself hoarse.

"I imagine Mr. Catherine has something or some things he wants." D's voice seemed even more silken compared to Justin's sandpaper tone, and his voice flowed between the rough edges of Justin's words.

"But I guess you don't have much of a say," Justin said, but he was quiet and seemed to be listening — to me? To D?

"Of course he does. He could kill you. He could go to the police. He could unite with Robert, and they could hatch plots and plans. He has all kinds of choices."

"If you want to see your wife again," Justin finished. I felt sorry for Tyler, who, from all descriptions didn't seem like a match for this slick, cruel man.

"I think Mr. Catherine realizes...what the reality of the situation is. Let's be respectful here."

I felt like my whole body, every cell, went into some kind of arrest, hoping this meant Catherine was alive and could be returned to me, even while the slow deep current moved against me.

My breath caught in my throat, and I realized I had made a kind of preliminary panicked sound, but I steeled myself.

"I'll do what you want. I'm more than willing, but I want some things, too." I nodded toward D in acknowledgement, but he stared straight ahead, swaying a little in the light breeze that had sprung up, which was somehow strong enough to move a grown man around in a swing.

"Can you answer some questions?"

"A question," Justin answered, interrupting me. "We can't stay here all day." He wasn't looking around, or seeming nervous, but the park was very exposed, and it surprised me that he would talk to me here at all.

"Okay. One question." I was quiet, trying to sort out what I wanted to know. What happened to Catherine? Where was she? Did she suffer? — Or rather, is she suffering? "How did you find her? I know how you knew who she was, how she was connected to Gewinn, but..."

"We started following him, Robert, to see what was up with him, after he *still* wouldn't pay us, and it was pretty boring shit, going to work, going to parties, going on business trips, getting his clients drunk, laid, that kind of shit.

"But, then, once or twice a week, he would get up really early – God, that was a bitch, following that bastard at 5:30 a.m., 6 a.m. Fucker never slept!- and drive down to the River Trail and just sit in his car, sometimes by the Big Dam Bridge, sometimes in one of the park entrances there, so he could see the path."

I turned in my swing so sharply the cold chains scraped against each other above my head. "He what?"

Again, he continued as if I hadn't spoken, "We knew about the affair, but we dealt with Tyler too soon, and I think the fact that we didn't have real details made him not take us very seriously, made our threats too empty, but they weren't empty. Tyler said it was a university faculty member who had left, and he probably said her name, but we were really paying attention to that shithead. So pretty soon, I saw he was watching this woman, um, your wife, I guess, when she went running in the mornings at the river. Shit, he led us right to her."

I exhaled audibly. I heard D turn toward me then, and the leather of his jacket creaked as he turned back to face the park when I didn't respond to his gaze.

"At first, we thought he was going there to, like, meet her or talk to her, but they never talked, and I don't think she even knew he was there. It was usually once a week that he managed to catch her. He would stay until he saw her, either when she got out of her car, or when she got back from running. It seemed like he just wanted to see her, and then he'd go. It was weird," he mused.

"Didn't she see his car?" I was confused, wondering if she was colluding somehow with this voyeuristic indulgence.

"He didn't park by her. He'd park up in that neighborhood right by the bridge and walk down, or he'd park in Murray Park, and watch her run by. It was pretty stalker of him. She didn't even notice him. So, we were pretty sure she wouldn't notice us till it was too late."

I winced.

"After that it was easy. I got her plates; we have a friend who's a cop, so we knew, but we didn't really need to know. We knew he was obsessed with her, and we knew where to find her. But when it came down to it, I knew having her name mattered.

"So, we went to him, me and Ryan, and we said we knew who Catherine Zrzavy was — what the hell kind of name is that, anyway? I mean, how do you even say it?"

"ZER-zah-vee," I instructed him robotically. "It's Czech. It means red-headed."

"Huh. Well, he was a little surprised that we knew that. I guess he was fucking clueless that we were following him pretty much everywhere he went. But he called our bluff. The guy is like made of steel or some shit."

"What bluff?"

"We told him we knew who she was, and we would hurt her if he didn't pay us a million dollars — he has it!" He said, defensively to my intake of breath. "That guy is made of money. His new salary is like more than that a year, and he has some kind of trust fund or inheritance that pads him. He can do whatever he wants. Tyler told us they have like three other houses."

I hadn't known the extent of Robert's wealth. It made me even angrier.

"Anyway, he wouldn't pay, so it was time to do something to her. We're not really kidnappers...Or we weren't," he corrected. "Now we are."

"Justin. You don't think you're being too sensitive, do you?" Asked D ironically, but without feeling.

Justin ignored the correction. "That fucker is a hard nut to crack, as my grandma used to say." He laughed to himself, some nostalgia taking over his features softening them to a mere parody of cold cruelty.

"Robert?" I asked.

"Yeah, but we'll get him."

I waited for D to pick up the thread. He was silent, but my mind was a cacophony. What did he mean, "We're not kidnappers"? Had they killed her, and they had more they wanted to do, to get? Or did they have her and wanted desperately to get rid of her? Had they killed her as an aside, as a task on a checklist they hadn't wanted to do but had done it like I took out the garbage, to get it over with, to move on to the next thing, to not be encumbered by it? My lively, beautiful wife, their annoyance. It took everything I had not to scream out to the affluent neighborhood so these rich residents could see who was sitting in their midst, quietly swinging, chatting on a cold winter day, about a murder, a devastating murder that was just was one of many. Or a cold, cruel, money-grubbing, marriage- and life-disrupting abduction. How would she come back to me? What would she be when I saw her again?

"Why don't you tell him what is next," said D, finally. It was not a request.

"So, here's what we want. We still want the million."

"We want two million," interjected D. It was the first time I had heard any desire or avarice in him. It was a faint note, like a woody taste at the end of a sip of cabernet.

"No, two million. Two million" agreed Justin. "And we're going to get it this time."

My stomach hurt, as if it were being twisted by two fists into a knot. "I'm to be part of this?" I'd never imagined this amount of "real money," as Ryan had called it.

"I told you all that stuff just now because you're one of us!" He reached over and patted me on the back, jocular, smiling to himself, but the pat was hard, intense. "You need to go to Robert. You seem like you can talk to him," said Justin. I looked at him to see if he were being sarcastic, if he had seen me with him that morning. "Make yourself useful. 'Cause here's the thing. We are going to frame him for the murder of your wife if he doesn't give us two million dollars in 48 hours."

I locked my knees as my swing was coming down, and my teeth knocked against each other painfully as my feet hit the dirt and the jamming rattled up my spine.

"And you're going to tell him and get the money for us."

"Why in the hell would I do that?" I asked. But I knew why, and I knew they knew.

"Because his being convicted for murdering Catherine will not make Mr. Catherine very happy, we think," said D, almost in a whisper. "It would all come out, wouldn't it?"

"How can you 'frame him?' I mean, how would that work? Do you think you are the CIA or something?"

"Just..." Justin hesitated, a slight frown of frustration and impatience crossed his features to be almost instantly erased. "Trust me. It won't go well for anybody. The money is better."

He paused, then spat out in a whisper that felt like a scream, "Why can't I just get my fucking money?" He looked past me and through D.

"To them, I am utterly nonexistent," said D.

"But if you don't frame him, won't they find you? Why would you let him buy his way out of this when it will become your problem?"

"Robert isn't the only person on my shit list. It's long. Very long." He laughed, in a guttural way, after drawing out the vowel in "long," lingering over it, enjoying it.

"And who's to say you didn't hire us to do something to your wife?"

I started in my swing, and my foot hit the ground painfully as I misjudged the distance in my shock. "What are you talking about?"

"You're talking to us in plain sight. You had a reason to get rid of her. The bitch cheated on you! You're just as guilty as anyone." He looked around openly, his face up to the trees and sky, demonstrating his willingness, his desire, to be seen with me. "I didn't come here to sit and chat with you all day, I came to lay groundwork, Mr. Catherine."

I was completely still, nauseated. My hands and fingers were frozen, too frightened to shake or fidget. He continued, "So, go to Robert, and tell him to give me two million, or I'll kill her and frame him — I can do it, and he knows it. If he thinks back over his behavior, he won't need convincing. I mean, I could kill him, but I think the murder rap will be worse for him. I want that fucking money. I've put in a long time on this job — I don't normally deal with stuff this long — and that shitbag Tyler owed me money, and I had to go through all of that shit. I want my fucking money." This refrain was a chorus of dark notes, murmured as he swung back and forth. "Plus interest. Plus penalties. And if you don't go to him, I guess things are going to get a lot more difficult for you soon, too."

"What do you think?" D asked, but it wasn't a question of my opinion. He was asking me how I was going to do it.

"You think he'll pay now, when all this time he wouldn't? Will he be intimidated now — when he wasn't before?" I could hear myself talking, but mostly I felt my insides contracting. I wanted to go home, be alone in our home, grieve my wife. Having to sit here on these childish swings was excruciating.

"I think he's scared, don't you?" D answered. His swing barely moved. His pale skin didn't seem to reflect the sun, but transmogrify it.

"Yes, I answered. "Won't you just kill him anyway?" It scared me that I had asked this aloud. I didn't want to expose myself to them as vulnerability, as an accuser.

"I do what I have to do," rationalized Justin. "But I don't enjoy it, and I don't do it for fucking fun. It's not fun. Money is fun. I want the money and I want to get out of this shit. And I cannot look like someone who doesn't get paid. I have to be paid. Everyone needs to know I will do whatever it takes to be paid." He stopped and looked at me hard before continuing.

"And when I tell someone to do something—" he twisted in his swing to face me directly, and he stooped a little in his seat to meet my gaze. "—they better fucking do it. But I'm tired of this. Jesus Christ, this Tyler shit is stretching on forever, and the guy is dead. I just want it to be over."

I turned toward D. He raised his eyebrows, but I couldn't tell what he meant.

"You want me to take this proposition to Robert? Convince him? So all of you can walk away from...from whatever's happened to my wife, and he can, too?"

"What's the alternative?" Asked Justin, as if he were trying to play D's role.

"Indeed," answered D.

I said nothing. I was afraid to say what the alternatives were, afraid they would kill me right there, and there would be an article in tomorrow's paper about a therapist found dead in Baker Park in Cammack Village.

But really, what were my alternatives? If I went to the police, the only thing that would come of it would be the public airing of my humiliation and Catherine's certain death, if she wasn't dead already — and then I may be implicated as a conspirator. If I went to Brooke, I had no idea what would happen. She was an officer of the court, not a therapist. Would she try to get me a deal with the police? Try to contact these killers herself? It scared me to think of her taking the modicum of control over this I still had out of my hands. Yes, Robert would suffer, but so would I, and so would the memory of Catherine. There was such slight possibility of protecting her; I clung to it.

As I thought of this, D slid his eyes at me, as if he knew what I was considering.

"Suppose he won't pay?" I asked.

Justin said, as if he'd been thinking his own, but parallel thought, "He'll pay."

"You've been overly optimistic about that before," cautioned D.

"And, you know what? I don't give a fuck anymore!" I looked around when Justin said this because it was so loud, so incongruous with the children's play area we were occupying. Was he yelling at D? He was standing with his swing banging behind him into the backs of his knees. We were still alone in the park, seemingly isolated in the neighborhood as well.

"Just tell him what you want him to do," prompted D.

"Find him, tell him what the deal is, that he's going to pay us the two million dollars, or we will frame him for your wife's murder. Even if he doesn't get the death penalty — which he will — he'll be ruined in the process. We can do it. It's not that hard. It's surprisingly not that hard," Justin laughed to himself.

"How should he get the money to you?" I felt like the grown up with a child making a wish list, trying to orient him on the practicalities. And yet I knew Justin was no child. In this world, in many ways, he was my mentor, my superior.

"When he agrees to it, tell him what's in here." Justin handed me a thin envelope. "It has the directions in it."

"Can I have my wife back?" – I couldn't hold it in anymore and a painful sob of desperation escaped me. Justin looked uncomfortable, annoyed. D grimaced.

"You can live." Justin said, and got up out of the swing and started off toward his car. After sitting a moment in silence, D followed him.

"We will see," said D. It was odd how comforting his sliver of a voice was at just that moment.

• • •

When I got back to the car, Lavinia was anxious, jumping from the back to the front and between the driver's seat and the passenger seat. She didn't calm down when I got in. Justin and D had already driven off. I was so close to my house, I felt like tomorrow the evil in Little Rock would erupt in my living room — as if it hadn't already.

I was trying to think on the drive home, through my anxiety and adrenaline, how to contact Robert again. I didn't want to call through his work secretary, because I didn't want her to mention to police two calls from the husband of the missing Catherine Zrzavy. He had said his wife was leaving town, so I thought I would wait until after dark and just drop in on him.

I drove home but couldn't get out of my car. I hated to face the house now — the days without Catherine were really weighing on me. Lavinia started to whine to get out and join Wesley, but I started the car again, backed out of the driveway, and then sat in the street until another driver, trying to pass by, honked me out of the way. I pulled in again and sat. I decided to get out her journals, to read more before it would be safe to go see Robert. I couldn't keep myself away from her thoughts; I had nothing else of her and nothing left to distract me. It seemed to be all I had left to discover about her.

I still feared what I would read about Robert in those pages. Robert who had caused all of this by fucking my wife, having a mess of a son who owed money to this gang, not paying them when they blackmailed him, not warning any of us in any real way, and continuing the charade even when it was clear they would call any bluff, eliminate any obstacle to getting this fucking money, I thought, echoing Justin.

I wished they would kill Robert. I hoped they would, that they would get his millions and then cut him down.

I now had real motivation to convey their message.

I walked back with Lavinia into the house and put food in their bowls for both dogs. I put water on for hot tea — I had some Czech liqueur Catherine liked to spike her tea with on nights like this — and picked up what I had called "the affair journal." I was afraid of it. I held it as if it were the object of the children's game, "hot potato." But I wanted to know. I wanted to understand what could drive Robert to follow my wife and watch her, weekly, what was the connection that made his vulnerability so palpable, that exposed her to her death?

With the kettle simmering, I sat down at the kitchen table, the journals piled in front of me, the one dark journal in my hands, and cracked it open toward the back.

January 2

> *I cannot continue to lie to H. It is an awful, isolating thing. And I fool myself thinking that I'm not alone because I am with Robert. I am not with anyone. I'm not with my husband who loves me because I am always thinking of Robert, and I*

am not with Robert because I am always stealing the time with him. Everything is always caving in on us, work, other people's demands, other people's suspicions. The secrecy of it, the lying. I'm betraying everyone I work with. So is he. We make these plans — ridiculous plans — to be together here or there, this weekend, that afternoon, and it's always vulnerable to the whim of another who has a claim to us, to him.

He says he loves me. I feel it when we are together, but that is the only time. The rest of the time, I'm desperate, lonely, unbelieving. What is a love that is only present when present? What a sad way to live when I share a home and a bed with a man who does love me. Whose love follows me? H does. He does. He does. And the claims on Robert are so real, so powerful, I never can stand up to them. He says he's not happy in his marriage, but he's utterly transparent to his family. They obviously know him very well. They suspect, I guess, and then make claims. To test him?

And Robert does not, DOES NOT, stand up to those claims. I can see it. He is a leaf in the wind. When his wife says he needs to be home by 5 p.m. because of whatever reason (such frippery at times. So bizarre.), he goes. HE GOES every time. He doesn't say, "No, I have a meeting," or "I'll get home as soon as I can." He tells me: "Well, I've got to go. Petra has the decorator coming over, and I want to see the swatches." I'm not kidding. Swatches. But when it is on me to lie to stay with him, I do it. I do it every time. I make it all possible. I tell H, when I can reach him, when he's not with clients, I have this meeting, or grading, or whatever. Whatever. I tell him something, and I stay.

But it's not just the daily little rejections by R that rankle, because he intersperses them with so many rewards, such goodness, such felt love. It's just the falseness of it all. Nothing is real in my life anymore. My job is fake because my boss is sleeping with me, so how can I know what I earned and what I "bought"? My marriage is fake because I'm sleeping with someone else. My romance is fake because I'm married to someone else. FAKE FAKE FAKE FUCKING FAKE.

I want to be real. I want to be seen. I want to move about in the world honestly, and with some kind of upright purpose, some reality. I must have it. If I cannot have it with H, I will leave him and have it on my own, but I won't have it with R in this world.

I don't know if I can stay, if I've already obliterated everything, or if it was already dead and dying. Such a slow, quiet, ridiculous sneaky death for a marriage, if it was. I don't think so, but I cannot ever really know doing what I'm doing.

So, I must do it. I must do it. I MUST DO IT. I must leave him. I must leave him, and I must tell H about it so I don't go back to Robert, which I will do if he wants me back. (I think he will — he won't leave her, but he won't want me to leave him, either.) It will be excruciating, so I have to find a way to shut the door behind me. I have to hurt H to stay with him in a way that is real.

I was googling the most ridiculous shit today (God, I hope the IT center doesn't ever pull my search lists! — could they be FOIA'd???), like "how to tell your husband about your affair," "How to end an affair," "What to do if your spouse is having an affair." Of course, the irony of being married to the family-

crisis expert has not escaped me. I suppose it won't escape him either. How awful for him. Dread.

So, as soon as I can, when I am with Robert, I will say goodbye to him. I will give myself that. That tiny, exquisitely painful thing. And then I will tell H, and there will be no turning back, no going back, no return to Robert. I will confess, and then I will be good, and I will be happy. I am writing it here. At least, it will be REAL. I hope I am happy with H, but if not, then not. But I will not be a faking liar anymore.

That was the last entry. The next journal, the clean slate, began later, with its strong desultory tone and no drama.

So, she had left him, I thought. She had made the decision, and while I was heartened by that, thinking that his narcissism drove him to follow her to the river because he could not stand being left, I felt a little let down, somehow, because she didn't write that she left Robert because of any passion or great feeling for me. She had written that she was tired of lying to me, that she knew I really loved her, yet her treatment of me wasn't passionate, the way her writing implied she was about him. In fact, I felt her passion for him fueled her leaving him. She hadn't made any such decision about me. Perhaps she had stayed out of inertia — but no, she wrote she was willing to be alone if it meant being happy and real.

I didn't know how to feel. I was reassured and hurt simultaneously. I shut the book. I didn't want to read more about their affair, not now. I kept the journals in the house this time, putting them back in a bag and then packing them under the television armoire in the living room, in the storage drawer there. I knew I wouldn't be able to keep

out of them eventually, but I wanted to parse out the knowledge and
the pain of them in endurable portions. I may have already overdone
it.

I tried to read the paper, a magazine, tried to watch television, but I
was restless, still, again. I got dressed for what I would wear to see
Robert, jeans, a blue-striped Oxford shirt, a winter vest, and I laid out
a coat. Then I tidied up the house, let the dogs out and in and fed
them. Finally, it was time to go to Robert's.

On the way over there I wondered what I would do if either of his
sons was at home. He'd told me he was shuttling his wife out of town,
but I didn't honestly know anything about his boys, Tyler's brothers.
They could be in school elsewhere, but who knew. I didn't want to
bring them any more pain than they were about to get if this went
awry.

I parked down the street, after nearly pulling into his driveway and
then circling the block, and walked up to the door inside his garage,
and rang the bell. Lights were blazing all over the house, so I was
expecting more than just Robert to be home. I waited a long time.
When I was debating whether to ring again or go home, the door
jerked open, and Robert stood in front of me in running clothes, with
a cellphone at his ear.

He didn't look surprised and motioned me in. In fact, he seemed
relieved, if not to see me, then maybe that I was not someone else. He
was unusually haggard and unkempt, with his leisure clothes roughly
slung on him, his T-shirt sweat stained at the neck and untucked. His
pants had a food — or alcohol? — stain on the left thigh. I couldn't
smell any liquor, and he had no drink in his hand. His manner
seemed blurred though. He didn't stumble or shuffle as he guided me

through into the kitchen in the back of the house, but his gait was not as purposeful. It lacked his typical ownership.

"Is your wife gone then?" The expansive kitchen wasn't dirty or messy, but it seemed like it was about to be untidy.

"Yes, she's en route, anyway." He sounded relieved, but he looked around as he said it, warily. "I'm here alone."

He offered me a drink from a kitchen bar, but I declined, though I wanted it. My mouth watered at the thought of it, and I swallowed.

"You're here with a purpose then?" He poured a scotch for himself. Two fingers.

I sat down and motioned for him to do so. I felt no awkwardness in hosting him in his own kitchen. He complied.

"I talked with Justin and D today. They have an idea of how this can all be resolved."

"Who is D?" he asked, and then dismissed the question with a wave. "Well, I imagine it involves my money." He sat forward in his chair and put his drink on the table.

"It involves many things." I thought of Catherine, her sly and biting sense of humor, and I tried not to think of her with him as I talked.

"What is it? What exactly do they want? What do they have to negotiate with? They can't be asking a ransom. I'm sorry," he motioned to me, and a sad and sour look crossed briefly over his features. "I really am sorry."

"They will kill her, and they will frame you for her murder if you do not pay them two million dollars by 5 p.m. Tuesday." He started to protest, his typical swagger seemingly injected in to him by the conflict. "They can do it."

"What do you mean they can do it? They killed her. There's got to be evidence. This is ridiculous."

"Do not say that again," I commanded. "It's not ridiculous. They have friends in law enforcement—"

"Of course they do." His manner was darkening. He started to fidget, but he didn't pick up his drink.

He slouched back in his chair. "This must be particularly triumphant for you, to be the bearer of this message." He fixed me with a gaze that made me think of how Catherine described him looking her in the eye at the luncheon.

I took a breath. "I would love to see you swing for this, honestly. The idea of you being held accountable for whatever has happened to her, what could happen to her is, well, seductive, if you'll let me use that word." He didn't blink. "So, no it's not 'triumphant' for me. But I do not want her name and reputation soiled with this or joined with yours in perpetuity. And, though I couldn't possibly care less about your slimy little life, I can't stand the thought of someone else dying."

I didn't tell him that there was a small, quiet voice in my mind telling me that it might mean something to Catherine that I could help someone she had loved. It made me feel pathetic, but I was desperate to feel I was doing something, anything for her. I wanted her back, but if that wasn't possible, I wanted something for her, something to come of this, something bigger than me. Even if it was for him.

"I am not responsible for what they did to her." He remained slouching when he said this, though his voice was forceful.

"Yes, yes, you are! How can you say that?! They warned you they would hurt her, so even if you didn't want to go to the cops with that, you could have told her more than you did that day at the banquet."

"That's debatable. I told you – "

I cut him off. "Either you're lying or you believe your own fictions, but I don't care anymore. Because when you used to drive down to the river to watch her running in the morning, you led those assholes right to her. They didn't know who she was until you pointed her out to them."

He seemed to lose about a third of his body weight then, wilting down into the wooden kitchen chair, looking down, his hands dropping to his sides.

"So pay them the money, because you're culpable. *You* are responsible. You may not have pulled any trigger, or whatever they might do to her, but you put her right in their path, you didn't warn her or anyone in any real way, and you did it all for your own reputation and your money. And this is her only chance."

He revived a little then, "And you? What about you? Are you the sainted victim in all this? You could have told the cops right away about the affair, about Tyler, but you didn't. And don't say it didn't come into your head. It must have. You keep saying you don't want her name dragged through the gossip mud, but who gives a shit about her down here? — Shit. I don't mean it that way, that she wasn't cared for. She was. She was..." He looked down, took a breath and kept talking before I could answer, "But it's not like she's well-known or any kind of celebrity."

"Like you?"

"Fuck you." The profanity blazed in the refined and gracious room, lighting it up, though he still seemed to sit in shadows. "You're not better than me because you're nobody. What you really don't want is for her name to be linked with mine, because it will humiliate you as a therapist...and as a man."

I said nothing. He stared at me, unflinching, but I didn't look away.

"I guess you'll have to cope with that, not me."

"What?" I asked.

"The simple fact that if you had told them right away, maybe you could have saved her life."

"She's not dead!" I yelled.

When I left his house moments later, both of us were filled with guilt, anger and resignation, I had an agreement that he would pay them the money, and I was to arrange the specifics with Justin and D. He had suggested my continued involvement, and though I was concerned about being watched by the police, I could see that he didn't trust himself to negotiate with them; I, too, was concerned he would renege if he were pushed into a corner, just to prove he was still in control. I imagined he was also worried they would kill him, but I didn't try to reassure him. What he feared was my ugly hope.

Day Seven

7

IT WAS MONDAY, AGAIN, but how different it seemed from the last Monday, only a week ago when we both rose to our normal workday routines. It seemed like years since I'd seen her face, heard her voice, and yet her dirty clothes were still in the hamper and our dogs were still looking for her in the house.

I wanted to talk to Catherine, to find her, to have her with me, and for the last time, I went to get her journals. I pushed aside the affair journal and the one she began after that and chose one at random. It was a dark gray Moleskin book, and as I held it, I remembered her keeping her entries in it about two years after we were married. I turned to a page and began to read.

March 2

> *I understand why people love spring. In the North, spring is just the miasma between winter and summer, when all the horrid snow melts and everything is a slushy mess and you wait for warmer weather to go to the lake and for the ground to dry. But here it is 68 degrees today — March 2! — and it's snowing in Pennsylvania. The sun is shining, and I am*

thinking of taking my groom to see daffodils at Wye Mountain this weekend, where I used to go with Amy and Daddy when I was small. Flowers in March. Flowering trees, white, pink, and azaleas! An azalea is a creature they don't know in the North, and certainly not in March. And I see I love it here.

I am surprising myself with my good mood today. I bickered with H at breakfast over who would walk Wesley, and I got stupid stink eye from the dean's secretary because I forgot to send her the RSVPs from the department for his "entre" lunch, but I sent them later and took it out of my mind, and the flowers on the trees, and the azaleas abloom on the campus and around the city, and the blue sky, and the honest-to-goodness spring breeze just perked me up. Up. Up. Up. And my opaque H cannot unperk me.

March 5

Beautiful day. Sunny. 59 degrees. Blue sky with those gorgeous puffy clouds that look like a fantasy. The ones I always take pictures of when I'm in an airplane.

We drove out to see the daffodils today in Wye. I don't know what I expected after all these years, I guess I remembered it differently, but it was kind of like a pretty Deliverance. *I shouldn't be so mean about my dear, sweet Arkansas. It's gorgeous, but it's so funny how you get about a minute outside Little Rock and it's really rural. Really. Really. We were probably about a stone's throw from a martini when we were there, but it felt ages away, which was lovely, and I wanted it.*

I wrote the other day that H is opaque. I've been thinking that for a while, but I guess I haven't said or written it. He's professionally opaque to his clients, and he's really good at it at other times, too. This reads like a complaint, which it isn't. He is so soothing and calming for me, and my mind is so racing and mean to me sometimes, I take his opacity willingly because it comes with that cool wave of love and acceptance — currents really. Or at least that's how I interpret it.

Today, among the daffodils, I was walking around the paths, and he took the camera off another way to take some pictures of it all. The whole thing is on the grounds of a little Methodist church out there, and I walked out toward a place where they had planted the bulbs in a cross shape. It was off just a little from the main field, among some trees, and I walked down there among them in my little left-from-grad-school wellies. I guess I was out of his view for a few minutes, and when I emerged, I could see him at the top of one of the little gold-covered hillocks frantic, casting around, walking haphazardly, trudging on flowers, the camera banging at his side. I started running to him, and he actually began to run to me. No blank, emotionless face. No even-keel rejoinder. No witty, but distant comeback. Fear. There was fear and relief. I asked him what was wrong, and he said: "I couldn't find you. I couldn't find you, and I just had this awful feeling that something was really wrong." I kind of chided him for thinking something so outlandish. "What could happen among all the daffodils on Wye Mountain??" He just put his head down, he was so relieved. I said a little defensively that I hadn't even been gone very long, and he said he'd been looking for me for almost 10 minutes, which I agree is a long time when you are afraid of something.

And some mean part of me felt a little grateful for that display, for that passion I saw there in the field with the flowers. We skipped dinner out and went home and I tore into him. I felt so close to him after seeing how much he loved me. I hated the fear for his sake, but I was relieved to know I could raise it in him. I must not raise it again. It would be too cruel. I will just remember this when I doubt. I will think about the flowers of Wye Mountain and his running to me, not caring about the camera, the people looking, his shoes in the dirt.

You are not supposed to pick the flowers, but as we were walking to the car, there was a bloom on the ground and I bent and pocketed it quickly. I'm saving it as a memento of this strange and awfully wonderful and wonderfully awful glimpse of what I mean to him.

I turned the page, and the dried and pressed daffodil slipped from the pages onto my lap. The pages that had pressed the flower were blank except for a few gold and brown smudges of pollen and oil from the petals. I picked up the petal delicately. It felt like papery ash, and I wanted to keep it whole, as she had done.

I could smell the field then, the sweat of my fear as I ran about in my fleece looking for her. I'd forgotten that day, which was curious; it was the single time she had scared me so deeply for her safety in all our years together, and in the past week, I'd been living those 10 minutes over and over and over. Was she telling me somehow that she was soon to emerge unharmed, mine again?

When Justin called my cellphone, I confirmed that Robert had finally agreed to pay. I told him there was nothing in the envelope about how he wanted the bills. He laughed.

"He's had the money for a month. He just wouldn't give it to us."

"What are you talking about?"

"Ask him if he doesn't have it. Did he bitch about having to get it or anything?"

"No..." I wheezed out the word.

"Good. This better go off. I don't like loose ends."

I wanted to put down the phone and go back to Robert's house with that baseball bat. After all his attempts to shame me, his refusal to give them money he'd had ready might have been the final die cast for her fate.

"Don't lose your shit," Justin had been saying my name into the phone for a few seconds.

"I'm just, I... I. Jesus."

Impatience surfaced in Justin's tone. "Do you have everything? He'll meet me? This can't go wrong or I'm going to take a torch to this whole fucking thing. You included." He hung up.

I sat in the chair in our dining room, with the silent cellphone pressed to my ear. All along I had been making a mistake I caution my clients against, which is to believe a person who repeatedly lies or obfuscates the truth.

"I bought what he was selling," I said to Wesley, who had come to sit attentively in front of me while I was on the phone with Justin. "I mean, I knew he was selling something — he's always selling something — and I bought it, too, even when I told him I wasn't, and I let him shame me into feeling so responsible for her actual death, when he is the one who got her kidnapped, and he is the one who got her—" I put my head down in my hands and tried to reorient my thinking, tried to focus on his unreliability and his lies. I had to go back and work out what he was to do to pay Justin and D, knowing he still may not try to wrest control of the negotiations, getting himself and/or me killed, and endangering Catherine further — and maybe even getting everything revealed in the process.

"I will have to follow him, and I will have to be ready to do what is necessary to get that money to Justin," I told Wesley. He watched me as I stood up, his eyes following me, but he didn't move to come with me. And part of me was thrilled at the idea that I had even more rationale to hurt Robert. Or to stop protecting him.

My phone lit up and vibrated: Brooke was calling. I reached for it, and then stopped, merely watching the screen pulse with light and her name. I let it go to voicemail, but she did not leave one. I was afraid to talk to her, afraid I would tell her too much, just fold and unburden myself, but I couldn't. Not when I was this close to saving my wife and our marriage.

"You're not yourself." I heard Catherine say, as if she were at my ear. I turned sharply, but, of course, she was not there. I smelled the Shalimar, as if she had just left the room. I heard the rustle of her workout gear, the swishing would envelop the house as she moved about after a run. Wesley stared at me, but Lavinia, in a corner, put her nose in the air and sniffed.

"I will see you soon," I said aloud to the perfume-scented air. The odor seemed to pulse, and then dissipate all together.

After I had paced through the dining room and kitchen for about ten minutes, I felt calm enough to call Robert and let him know what he needed to do. I decided I would not confront him about having had the money; I didn't want him to see me as any more of a combatant. If I had to get close to him to get control of the money, it would be easier if he felt he were still my puppeteer.

"They want you to bring the money in cash tomorrow to Burns Park."

"It may take me longer than that to get the—"

"No."

"No, what? It's not something that's yes or no. I have the money, and yes, I can get it, but I..."

"No one cares about your issues getting the money. I don't want to know about it or what you have to do. That's your problem to solve." I was teetering on the edge of my resolve already because of his chronic need to perseverate on each and every little point of this macabre process, to continue to try to control me.

"I'm merely..."

"Get the money and take it to Burns Park."

"Okay...but should I call you if there's a problem getting it?"

"No, just go there without it. How's that?"

"I won't have to go there. In that case, I suspect they'll come to me."

"Exactly. Do you know where the dog park is in Burns Park? Near the soccer fields?"

"In Burns Park, not the Murray Park dog park?"

I felt a painful twinge, wondering if he'd watched Catherine with our dogs in Murray Park.

"Not Murray Park," was all I could say.

"All right. I'll find it. I'll find it."

"It's across the river, kind of, from the Rebsamen Golf Course. There's road access to it, I think it's called Tournament Drive or

Road, something like that. Anyway, that's not exactly where you're going. The road runs along the river there, south of the dog park, going east and west. If you follow it east, it turns north, and goes up a hill. At the turn, before the uphill section, there's a public restroom."

"Is it a building or a port-a-potty or what?"

"It's a building, gray cinderblock with a blue roof. All the facilities in Burns Park have those blue roofs. You can see them from across the river in Little Rock, in the soccer park, and this one in particular."

"So, I'm supposed to meet a guy in a public men's room? That sounds like they'll be able to spin this 18 different ways."

"Meet him with the money, cash, tomorrow at 10 a.m."

"Ten? Yesterday you said 5 p.m."

"It changed."

He sighed. "Did they say what denominations to get?"

"I asked him that, and he was vague, something about whatever you have is fine. What does he mean?" I couldn't resist testing him — or maybe I was just giving him a chance to be honest with me one last time.

"I suppose he's talking about cash on hand. I keep some for..." he hesitated, and I was gratified that his lying wasn't always so smooth and seamless.

"Ransoms?"

"Various business and personal things, but not two million. I'll get what I've gotten in the past. It'll arouse less suspicion."

"Whatever you think," I paused, resisting the mollification that was seeping into my psyche. I wanted to hate him too much to believe in him — but I had to.

"You need to be in the bathroom with black backpacks with the money when they come in the men's room at 10 a.m.," I directed.

"Do not be late. You know as well as I do that they are not kidding around. If they don't get the money now, well...I don't need to say it.

"No. This is it."

"Don't think that you can do anything now but what they say." I hung up, without waiting for an answer.

I called Chuck next and asked to borrow his car. He didn't ask anything except when I needed it. "Right away," I said. "I'll just drive over there and leave my car with you to use. I'll return your car with a full tank," I promised, wondering if I would live to give it back to him.

"God! I don't care about that. You know that!" He sounded worried, restrained, angry, even.

"I'll explain it someday, if you want me to."

"Will I want you to?"

"No. And you'll probably figure it out without my doing so if things happen as I think they will."

He was quiet.

"Chuck?"

"Yes, yes, of course you can borrow it right now. I just...you didn't say how you 'hoped' things would happen, so I'm worried."

"Don't worry. There's no need to worry. Things are bad enough now that if they get worse you won't even notice."

When I got to his house in Cammack Village, I handed him the keys to the Subaru.

"No dogs with you today? You know I don't care if you have them in my car. Our dogs are in with us all the time."

"No, not today."

He looked me over, his face riddled with concern, and showing a hint of fear. His left eyebrow twitched, the same way it used to twenty-five years ago before a big exam.

"Are you okay? Just tell me if you're okay."

"Yes, I am. And I will be fine. I'm actually trying to take some precautions today; that's why I need your car. I need to not be recognized so easily."

He looked around, down the street, and up the other direction.

"Do you think you were followed here?"

"I don't. No." He relaxed. "Are you worried that I'm paranoid, or that I really was followed?" I smiled. It didn't seem to appease him.

"I'm just worried in an all-around, this-whole-thing-is-totally-fucked-up way." He paused. "I'm used to my clients not telling me things, but not my friends."

"I'll tell you everything, really, everything, tomorrow," I said.

"Brooke may be trying to call you. She's got some procedural things to check in on you with, and I think she has some updates for you," he said, a helpless timbre in his voice I hadn't heard before.

"I'll talk to her tomorrow, too. I promise."

"Is this about — ?" He stopped himself. I looked at him, impatient.

"Is what about what?"

His lower jaw edged out and he bit his upper lip, scraping his teeth back and forth across his lip.

"I know about Robert," he said, but he would not look at me.

I tried to put the car in park but missed in the unfamiliar sedan and left it in neutral, and then was confused when it started to roll backward. I braked and finally got the right gear. I got up and out of the car.

"What did you say?" I asked him in a whisper. Then, with more trepidation, "Does Brooke know?"

"I know about the affair Catherine had," he said, ignoring the second question, which I was afraid was an affirmative, and panic began to set in. My bifurcated mind began to work on both levels: trying to focus on him, machinating in the background about damage control.

"She told me about it not long after she confessed to you. I think you were still in counseling."

"Didn't she have her own friends?" I asked. My resentment about letting him in to my marriage's secrets was palpable, but he didn't blanch.

"She was my friend, you know; I met her through Brooke, of course, but I always considered her a friend, not just your wife. But she didn't confide in me, not like that. She told me because she was asking me what to do. I think she thought you'd told me, and she wanted to know how to understand better where you were with everything."

"What did you tell her?"

"I didn't know what to do. I'm not a poster child for marriage or fidelity," he laughed, but it was raw and empty.

"I don't understand. What to do about what?"

"About the fact that you never really forgave her."

"But I—"

"I don't know where you were or what was going on, but she said she felt like you hadn't really forgiven her, and that there were still barriers between you two that she thought weren't good. She said she tried to talk to you about hard things after the affair was over, and you were receptive, but she felt it was kind of...what's the word, 'rote,' like these were the things you were supposed to do, but that there wasn't real feeling behind it. She didn't want to go back into the affair, but she felt vulnerable to it because she still felt such distance between you. She felt she could go back to Robert, and it scared her, because she wanted that door to close permanently, or your door to her to open permanently, and neither thing was happening. The ambiguity was stressing her out. And she hated her job."

He finished in a big breath, and then he looked at me and held my gaze, like an accusation, I thought.

"I can't believe she would tell my best friend all of this and not tell me," was all I could think to say.

"I can't believe my best friend didn't tell me all this had happened to him, especially after everything you've seen in my marriages."

"I couldn't manage it," I confessed.

"Well, I don't think you were managing it anywhere," he said. He shook his head, and I felt the implications. Somehow, he knew this had to do with Robert. He probably knew more about Robert, his son and his troubles than I did, even now. We'd all had our own little pool of truth, of perspective, of belief, and, separated, those waters made no current that could push against the inevitable tide that had washed Catherine away.

"You know, I came and picked her up that night at Gypsy's," he said as if going down a list of things he'd kept from me. "That night you fought about the LSU job. She stayed here and talked it over with me and Nicole — that was right after she and I had gotten married. Cath wasn't friends with Brooke anymore really. Nicole told her to 'suck it up, Buttercup!' and she decided to take the UALR job."

I stared at him, feeling like the walls were closing in, trying to process all this old information from my marriage all these years later.

"She didn't tell you that's where she'd been?" Chuck asked. I shook my head. "You didn't ask? Jesus. You're even worse at marriage than I am." He looked down and squared his jaw and sighed. "I haven't told Brooke any of this; I was hoping you would. You're handicapping her — and yourself — by keeping secrets. But I think she's figuring it out without you. You need to call her."

I turned and got in his BMW, a compact, late model four-door sedan. He always seemed too big for the car, but when I got in, I felt small with all of his seat and mirror settings. He laughed when he saw how low I sat in the driver's seat, but he sounded mirthless and distant.

"Yeah, go ahead and mess up all my carefully calibrated seat specifications. You're such an asshole sometimes." I continued moving and adjusting the seat with the power controls, ignoring his attempt at humor, and he shut the door on me, hitting the top of the car twice, indicating he was ready for me to leave. I looked and backed out onto his street. I drove straight over to Robert's and parked down the block, turning off the motor and trying to see the cars in his driveway. I'd called him at home, so I knew he had been there earlier. I looked around, hoping I didn't seem too conspicuous in the middle of the day. Hillcrest residents seemed nervous in their neighborhoods with all the recent home break-ins, the smash-and-grab crime of Little Rock daily life. I tried to think of a plausible reason I might be sitting in my car here in case of confrontation, but before I could come up with something, Robert's car backed out of his garage, and he drove off down the street away from me. I started my car and tried to keep up with him.

He drove downtown and into the ramp of the Regions Building, to his office, I assumed, though the large bank in the base two floors was also a possibility. I circled the block and then followed him in, grabbing my ticket and hoping I had enough cash to get out. I slowly wound my way up the levels, not wanting to drive past him while he was walking in.

But I could hear Catherine, almost as if she were in the car: "You never have cash. That's so ridiculous. You need cash, just a little. Someday you're going to call me begging to come rescue you from your cashless debtor's prison." I took deep breaths to keep from turning around to look for her. "I'll see you soon," I said aloud.

I found Robert's car in the bank-customer-parking-only spots in the first couple of levels and looked for a place to park to watch for his return. It could be hours if he were going to his office, but I had nothing else to do. I was too afraid of him failing me to let him out of my sight now. I was also nervous about not having cash to get out of the deck. Would they take a debit card? I hadn't noticed. If I were following him and got stuck at the exit, it would be over. My heart was pounding.

"Okay," I didn't say her name, but I was admitting to Catherine that she had been right. The sleep deprivation, the alcohol, the sleeping aids from Sandra had accrued in my system, and I knew I wasn't myself. The edges blurred from encroaching panic. I took another Xanax, though, to calm down, and then I walked toward the elevator, and took it to the first level of the building, hoping to find a cash machine and quickly get back to the car before Robert returned to his. If he was getting a lot of cash, which I didn't believe he was doing, it would take him some time. I looked around for stairs to take back instead to avoid running into him on the elevator. In the stairwell, I could only go to the second floor of the Regions Building and exit, make my way inside down to the first floor, and then return to the second to locate the cash machine. Finished, I found the stairs again and went up a flight to my car.

I confirmed Robert was still within the building as I walked past his car and moved as quickly as possible to get inside Chuck's BMW. I adjusted the rearview mirror so that I could see every car that passed behind me. There was no other way out than to go by me before taking the exit route down the other side of the ramp to get to the exit pay booth. I slid down in the seat to minimize my presence and watched the mirror. I counted the minutes between passing cars, putting my hand on the ignition every time I heard a motor in that high-powered low gear necessary to proceed slowly up the ramp's never-ending hill. Then I started averaging the minutes between cars and noting if a car was "early" or "late." I wished I had brought a dog.

At the point where the averages had reached about 3 minutes, an "early" car turned out to be Robert's. I'd been waiting about 45 minutes. I started the engine as soon as he went by and backed out slowly, staying behind, though in the strange car, I thought I wouldn't be immediately recognized. I took the baseball hat off the seat, and put it on, lowering it as much as I could over my forehead. It wasn't sunny, so I hadn't brought sunglasses. I thought wearing them would attract too much attention.

I turned into the pay gate area just in time to see Robert glide through a monthly parking permit lane. I quickly grabbed my ticket and cash for the attendant.

"Two dollars and 25 cents, please," said a man with a thick accent. "Luis" read his uniform above his heart. I handed him a ten-dollar bill and told him to keep the change, he hesitated, but I drove off, displeased at the way I was calling attention to myself.

The street at the exit was a one-way, and "right-turn only" signs were posted at the sidewalk, but Robert went straight into an alley that ran between a brown brick building of several stories and a monthly contract parking lot. I had to wait for a car to pass to follow him, but I was nervous doing so. Surely, he would notice the car behind him, though I imagined frequenters of this garage often used this trick. Still, I turned right onto the one-way, and left to go around the block. I was fortunate to see his car ahead traveling west on Third Street.

I turned on the radio, and then turned it off to clear my head and stay focused and gripped the steering wheel. I kept casting glances in the side and rearview mirrors to see if anyone was following me, or Robert, but I didn't see anyone. It wasn't like them to take any chances, Justin and D, but I knew they had grown bored and frustrated with the whole thing. They may be hoping Robert would object again so they could end it with their natural inclinations unchecked.

I wasn't feeling quite so laissez-faire about him, though. I hadn't seen him go in or out of the bank, so I didn't know if he was carrying anything either direction. He could have used the customer space to gain quick access to his office. Or he could have gotten money in his office; I didn't know where the cash was, and it would probably be safer in his office than at home. Maybe he didn't want his wife to know about the withdrawn funds.

I had to stop thinking of possibilities, though. I tried to focus on what I observed and follow him closely enough not to lose him — as I had the last time when D had found me.

Third Street morphs into Markham leaving downtown to the West, so I thought he may be on his way home, but just before the neighborhood changed, he turned north and doubled back to

Broadway and turned north again, taking the bridge into North Little Rock, and then traveling west.

When he reached Burns Park, I tried to hold back, as January wasn't prime park time, but there were too many options and turns in the park that I was afraid I would lose him, or he would find me coming at him if he turned around. He drove slowly by the golf course, and then down toward the dog park. At the bottom of the hill, just as I'd directed him, he slowed and stopped in the middle of the road when he saw the park restroom building on the river. I was afraid it would be locked in the cold weather, but as I coasted by, I saw him trying the men's room door. It gave as I passed out of view.

I turned around in the dog park lot and decided I'd need to be satisfied with this vantage point, though it was too far and on the wrong side of the building to see him come or go. Scanning the park, I saw no cars that looked like D's, though I didn't know what Justin might drive. No cars drove by.

It was about 20 minutes before Robert emerged; though I just saw his car exit and travel back up the hill. This time, he went home, after driving through Starbucks on Broadway once he was back in Little Rock. I waited hours until the lights were all off in his house and was about to go home to let out the dogs, but I was afraid to leave.

"Chuck?" I asked into the phone.

"Yeah. Man, I'm glad to hear your voice."

"Can you go let out Wesley and Lavinia? I can't... I can't get away."

"You're okay? You need me? I can come anywhere, do anything."

"I'm fine. I mean it. I just need to be where I am right now. I thought I would get away to come home for 20 minutes or so, but I don't think that's a good call. You have the key? I think there's one in..."

"No, I got it. I'll go check on things for you. It's...what time is it? Sorry, I was busy with a transcript."

"It's 9:30."

"Cool. I'll go right now."

"I'm sorry to bother you."

"You know it's no bother. I'll be glad to go check on the kids and make sure everything's okay." He sounded penitent, regretful, maybe of not telling me what he knew about Catherine all along, or maybe for telling me this morning.

"Be careful, Chuck. I'm sorry to ask. I just, don't have anyone else to call. It's just you're driving my car, and you'll be at my house."

"I'll take Jill's car. It's cool."

I regretted not going to Starbucks myself. Though the anxiety had kept me alert, I was starting to feel the kind of tired I felt when driving long distances, and knew I would pass out without being able to stop it, only realizing I had been asleep when I woke. I was parked closer to Robert's house than I liked, but it was near a house with a for-sale sign that didn't look lived in. I wanted to be able to hear as well as see him leave, and as I continually dozed and woke, dozed and woke, I was grateful each time I saw the same cars in the garage.

Chuck called me around eleven.

"Is it okay for me to call you?"

"Of course. Is everything all right?"

"Yeah." He paused. "Am I paranoid if I thought someone was following me? You said you were nervous about my taking your car there."

"What kind of car?"

My question seemed to scare him, and he hesitated.

"Um, a black, Lexus I think. One of those not-SUVs they make."

"Okay. Yeah."

"This is serious. Do you think I was being followed?"

I was completely awake now. Robert's house was still dark, and everything looked the same as it had.

"What happened? Everyone and their dog has one of those kinds of cars these days."

"I know, I know. It was after I left your house. I turned to go back down Rockwood to take it over to Greenwood to get home, which isn't really a common traffic pattern."

"No, but people in those neighborhoods go that way a lot to avoid Cantrell." Why was I trying to talk him out of it? To protect him? Or was I making him feel safer than he was?

"Yeah, but it was weird, because that car was behind me when I turned right onto Rockwood, which is no big deal, but then I got behind one of those infernal golf carts people drive around up there, and instead of going straight on Rockwood, I turned onto Pine Valley and had to go back down Sunset to pick up Greenwood. They were still following me two blocks after that."

"Right behind you? Right on your tail?"

"Not up my tailpipe or anything, but, yeah, right behind me."

"Did it feel aggressive to you?"

He laughed, but it was dry and dead sounding. "I don't know the difference between an aggressive tail and a more, what? Polite tail? Is this acceptable following behavior?"

"I only wanted to understand if you were in any danger."

"Shit. Shit. Shit." He exhaled for a long time.

"Look, it sounds like you're okay. They probably figured out you did just what you did: walked the dogs. Maybe they're looking for me. Which means they don't know where I am now. They'll find me soon enough, but don't go back."

"Yeah, I was going to tell you, I brought Wesley and Lavinia back with me," said Chuck.

"Oh, my God. Thank you. Why didn't I just leave them with you when I brought over the car?"

"Well, I made the decision before I got freaked out by the car up my ass, because I wanted to know they were okay, and I wanted you to know they were, too. I have no idea what you have in mind, but I didn't know if your house was going to be off-limits any time soon, so when I was leaving, I just loaded them up."

"If anything happens to me, will you keep them, or find them homes?" I asked it before it occurred to me to stop myself for his sake.

He didn't pause before he answered. "We'll keep them. If you can't be with them, I can't stand for them to go anywhere else. You know...you should call Brooke."

"If you know something, just tell me. I don't like her. I don't want to talk to her now."

"I knew you didn't like her. That's funny — she reminds me so much of Catherine, not just because they were friends. Anyway," he spoke quickly to override the interjection I was about to make. "I've been telling you to call her because they've ruled you out officially as a suspect, not just because of the phone stuff, but because they found Bridge footage of her being abducted."

"*What?!*"

"Not the actual footage, but vantage points from enough cameras at the right times to know what cars were in the area and where she was when and where she wasn't when she should have been. You were still at home then, and your neighbors corroborated this."

"What are they doing about it?" I thought then about just going home, giving up, letting them take everything over. I wanted my dogs and my own bed so much. I wanted to be there when my wife came home.

"Now that is something they won't tell us, but they sounded optimistic," he said.

She was alive! I knew it. I could feel it all along.

"So maybe...whatever you're doing, you can stop doing it?"

"I'd love to, but I think I need to see it through," I said, and I hoped that meant I would also be seeing my wife the next morning.

"Brooke has some information she'd like to give to the cops — not from me. If she knows anything, she found it out herself, but I think she wants to talk it over with you. You need to call her."

I just nodded and we ended the call. I decided to get the dogs from Chuck early the next morning for a true family reunion. But I wasn't going to talk to Brooke until I had taken care of everything I could, until there wasn't anything to hide or any need to tell.

Day Eight

8

AGAIN, I DIDN'T SLEEP, cramped in the car, trying to stay down so it would look like an empty sedan in front of an empty house. In the morning, I had eaten the few provisions I'd brought and needed a bathroom again, after driving over to Kroger during the night. It seemed better to go earlier rather than later, so I drove to the Starbucks on Kavanaugh, where Robert and I had met only days before. I walked in at 5:45 a.m., used the bathroom and ordered a venti black coffee, picking up several of the bakery offerings they had on offer and a *New York Times*. I was gone about 25 minutes, but one of his cars was gone when I returned to Robert's street.

"Fuck it!" I said and drove over to Chuck's, parking in his driveway and walking to his carport kitchen door without expending the energy to check the neighborhood or street for who might be watching. I knocked and waited. When he came to the door, his messy hair and slack face appeared to have been awake only since my knock. He pushed open the screen door toward me, and as I stepped back I asked for the dogs.

"What's up?" he asked, ignoring my manic appearance, but he seemed to know I wouldn't answer. He leashed Wesley and Lavinia and walked them out to the car in his lounge pants and Arkansas Razorbacks T-shirt. My nerves were so jangly, I couldn't stand to explain what I was doing. I thanked him and got his renewed promise to take care of them if...

• • •

When I got back to Robert's, I wondered if he'd seen me and had been waiting to make an escape, but I was too tired to get upset about it, and there was nothing I could do. If they were keeping tabs on Robert, then they'd have seen me by now. But I didn't want to tempt any altercations, violent or not, by putting myself in the neighborhood they were so clearly patrolling. I ate two of the scones and drank half the cooling coffee and thought about where I could go to stay safe until about 9:15 or so, when I was going to drive back to Burns Park to wait for the handoff.

I dawdled, hoping he would return. But when a neighborhood woman walking her dog looked into the car with concern, I waited for her to round her corner and started the car. I drove down Cantrell Hill to the Waffle House in the Rebsamen neighborhood and went inside, ordering proteins — bacon and eggs — to answer the sugar load of the last hour, and more coffee.

I had my newspaper and sat in a booth, listening to traffic and pulling my eyes through the columns of type. I couldn't concentrate, but I was happy to have somewhere to rest my gaze. I was done scanning for anyone suspicious or threatening; I had reached my limit. I remembered the scene at the end of the *Sopranos,* which Catherine and I had watched together, when Tony sits in a restaurant booth with his family and everything goes dark. Is that how it would feel?

When I was in my teens, I had nightmares that had made me feel the same way as I did watching that episode. It was the way I'd felt since Catherine disappeared. Or perhaps it had started bubbling to the surface when she confessed her affair to me. In my dreams, I had been looking out of eyeholes, so incredibly conscious of both being in a body and being separate from that body. I watched two people, me and my mother, from behind in what looked like a sitcom set, like maybe in *Father Knows Best* or that kind of thing, and in my dream, my own skin was in color, but everything else was black and white. I watched myself and my mother, and I knew something horrible was about to happen to them, to me and to her, something so incredibly painful and terrifying, but I didn't know what it was, and I could not warn myself. I always woke up before anything did happen, completely afraid, feeling the world was too ominous to stand.

As a therapist, I had heard other children of alcoholics talk of similar dreams, the deep foreboding, the anguish over the horror of what might happen was worse than many things that did happen. Now, I seemed to be living that nightmare, and I wondered if it had just been a premonition — a prophecy — of my future all along, a black-and-white sitcom shadow cast by the long rays of my future pain. That morning, I had never seen a place more terrifying than that Waffle House. Every movement from the patrons and the wait staff felt staged, warning me something wasn't right. I was as though someone, some version of myself, was watching, wanting to scream, to tell me to escape — or how to escape — and I couldn't hear, but I got the message of danger. Again, or still, I smelled Catherine's Shalimar. The whole restaurant was awash in sunlight, but I sat in a darkened corner.

I dumped my garbage from my breakfast and drove to the Little Rock-side Arkansas river access at Murray Park, about a mile from the Big Dam Bridge. I knew it was foolish to be isolated, but I felt I would explode out of my skin if I had to keep it together in public. Anyway, there wasn't really anything I could do to keep them away from me if they had decided to knock me down next.

I was parked near the boat launch, facing the river. About 20 minutes after I arrived, motion in my rearview mirror caught my eye. It was a black thin shape, moving through the grass. D. My breath quickened. The dogs didn't react to him; they were watching two heron in the Arkansas River.

I unlocked the sedan doors before he approached, and I leaned over and opened the passenger door for him while clearing the seat of the night's stakeout detritus. He was still encased in leather. It seemed a little crisp for the cold morning, but he looked impervious to anything like climate.

"How do you think things will go today?" He was looking across the river at the blue restroom facility where Robert was to meet Justin. He left his door open.

"I imagine that's up to you."

"You are probably a good therapist, are you not, Mr. Catherine?"

"Please call..."

"But I like to call you that. I mean, isn't that how I know you? You were — you are — married to her."

"It's painful."

"I imagine." He was imitating me. "It's really up to Robert, and to Justin, and you. You are the actors in this, aren't you?"

"Actors?"

"I didn't mean that you are playing a part, though I imagine you are in some ways. I guess the word has multiple applications. And, of course, anyone who is married plays parts over the years, plays at being faithful, plays at forgiveness..." He tapered off, but the words hung in the air about me.

"I just want Robert to hand over the money. I don't know what else I can do to make that happen."

"Yes, he was wily and got away from you this morning."

"He is wily." That word was slick and slimy in my mouth.

"You must hate him."

"Of course, I hate him."

"Well, I believe Justin is going to kill him today. I think it will make a lot of problems for Justin, because Robert is well-known, and the police won't let the case go as easily as Justin would like to think."

"Like they have Catherine's?"

"But they haven't, my friend, and you should call your attorney more often. They aren't bothering you because they suspected Ryan right away, but they couldn't make the connections between him and her, and now they are looking at Justin. But Justin is determined to make Robert the suspect, just because he is tired of being thwarted by him. It's an intricate exchange of grudges and power plays. These boys were foolish driving around, following her for several days before it happened, in places like the Bridge where there were cameras — but so was Robert, for months."

I tried not to think of Robert going to the meeting point, afraid D could read my mind. I cast about for something else to say or talk about. But he didn't wait.

"If he decides to kill Robert today and succeeds, they will descend upon him faster than he can throw them off his trail."

"Do they know about Catherine?"

"About her and Robert? I don't think so. The police know Justin as a suspect in many other offenses. I wouldn't be surprised if they had looked into him by force of habit the day she disappeared, and he made mistakes, as people do."

"Catherine certainly did."

"She did, but not one that deserved her punishment."

"Why are you talking like this? Didn't you do this?"

He turned so suddenly to me, I didn't see him move, but when I looked over, he was facing me full on, leaning toward me. His paleness was unbroken by freckling or sun, or even, it seemed, blood. He reminded me of Catherine on the deck that day, unable to hear me.

"Why are you telling me all this?" My voice was broken. I heard it as if listening to someone else speak.

"I'm only voicing what you already know. You are not a stupid man." He grimaced. Maybe it was a smile. "What are your plans today?" His voice was colder than usual, with less silken purr.

"I wanted to make sure Robert went to the meeting, but I lost track of him, like usual, so I guess I'll go and park somewhere nearby and watch what happens. Unless...?"

"Unless?"

"Unless you think I should do something else."

"I have no opinion. But I have a favor to ask you."

I nodded; he took it to mean to ask the favor, but I meant I would do what he said.

"I thought I might go with you, and...watch. I share your curiosity."

I nodded again and started the car to drive to Burns Park on the other side of the gray, rowdy waves in front of us. Somehow, it was almost 9 a.m. D's door shut with the force of my turn out of the parking lot.

I went back through downtown, over the Broadway Bridge to the park, taking the same route Robert had taken yesterday. I wasn't sure where to put the car so we could both see. There was a beat-up gray Chevy pickup truck in the parking lot to the southeast of the restroom building. The parking lot ran at an angle from the shelter to the river to the south. To the west was more park, including the dog-run areas and the soccer fields. Lavinia whined, hearing even this far away the scampering puppies, the play. In my stomach I felt the hard knot of everything I'd eaten that day.

"Pull in there. Park behind the pickup," directed D. I looked over to confirm, but he looked ahead, and the car went there, as if directed by his gaze. "He doesn't know this car. Did you tell Robert you were switching vehicles?"

"No." The way he said "vehicle" made me hope to never hear the word again.

"Ah, you switched to follow him. Well, then they are both unaware. Unaware of things they should be aware of. This is dangerous, isn't it?" He smiled.

"It was for Catherine. I suspect it will be for me."

I froze, thinking this is a very good time and place for me to be killed — the cold river ahead to dump my body, the truck protecting us from road or a direct line of sight from the path. Perhaps that was why I wanted the dogs with me. They seemed to be on a different plane than D, unresponsive to him. He didn't acknowledge them either.

"I'm asking you if there is something you think should be taken care of. Something you've left undone. Some loose end someone could find about all this."

"No, nothing specific. I've just..."

"Okay, then. That is all I wanted to know. We should be quiet now, and wait," said D.

"We can't see the building from here..."

"We won't need to. Just watch."

I stared at the water, feeling very cold, at the same time I could still feel the residual warmth from the heated seats on my thighs and lower back. I cracked the car door and threw up in the parking lot.

"It's best to have gotten that over with. Something like that might be noticeable." D remarked. His voice was patient, but he had turned to look back toward the road, with the limited view he had over the bed of the truck. His body seemed taut instead of just sinewy for the first time, but he wasn't nervous. Out of the corner of my eye, I thought I saw Catherine's strawberry blonde hair cascading onto his jacket. I turned and saw only him and his black leather.

There was excitement in his voice when he announced Robert had arrived. A moment later, I heard the car pull into the lot. I couldn't see it once it came through the driveway, but I could hear it parking between the truck and the restrooms. When it left D's view, he settled down in his seat and gazed ahead, intent, focused, like distilled anticipation. He looked paler than ever. Then Robert got out of the car, walking around the truck to angle back toward the building, as if he were walking up from the river. I heard low voices after the car's engine was turned off.

I glanced at the clock. It was 9:36 a.m. Justin was to arrive in 24 minutes for the money. I listened, but heard only the scraping of the shelter door, and then nothing except the dog's breathing, not D's, not my own. When I checked the clock again, the time had not changed.

He followed my gaze to the clock. "Time is so unwieldy at such moments," remarked D impassively, but he was once again excitedly coiled in his seat, as if he could shed his leather and the car altogether any second. He was voicing my thoughts, from a cold and deep part of my mind.

Several minutes later, D's whisper was sharply edged when we heard Robert emerge from the bathrooms: "Slide down. Now." I complied, though he didn't, and I heard footprints approach the rear of the BMW. There was no pause before they receded, as Robert walked back toward the restroom building.

I heard his feet quickly pace the stairs and the scuff of a door against the dusty pavement, and a quiet thud, and then silence. It was 9:39 a.m. D and I waited. He may have been electrified with the thrill, but I was exhausted and so anxious I could feel the stress stiffening my neck and shoulders, freezing the muscles into knotted bands. I wondered if Robert would emerge from the building, or if he could endure the wait patiently, silently. But we heard nothing. No cyclists or joggers passed by on the path either.

Finally, at 9:58, a second car pulled in the lot.

One of us said as a kind of confirmation, "Justin."

I slid down in my seat again, but Justin must have parked right by the building, because we almost immediately heard his feet on the steps and the scrape of the door opening and then shutting. Now I really smelled Shalimar. I looked up and gasped.

Catherine, looking strangely as she had on the deck in my dream, was walking into the shelter as well. Her running clothes looked fresh, as they had when she left the house, her hair washed and wavy, earbuds in her ears. She did not look around. She wasn't handled by Justin. She walked, solitary, toward the bathroom, nearly glowing. I was so relieved to see her, but my fear for her froze me to my seat. I squeezed my eyes shut so that when I opened them, I would know she really was there, but when I focused again on the shelter, I had missed her. Had she gone in? I turned to the dogs. They weren't looking in her direction, but Lavinia's nostrils were twitching. She made a low whining moan and cast her gaze about.

I heard nothing. I wanted to run into the bathroom, to make sure that the money was exchanged, that Catherine was safe. I had seen her! She was there! Alive! I hadn't believed it, but I had seen her, I had smelled her perfume. It would only be moments now. I thought of the scent of the preserved daffodil that fell from the pages of her journal and rubbed my fingers together as if I had the dusty, papery petals between them. The scent became more than a memory around me.

Justin would get the money, and I would get my wife, our triumphs would be at Robert's expense, and now it was only minutes away. I kept watching the clock, and it seemed as if the minute would not move from 10:02 to 10:03. Just as it did, we heard a loud crack or pop come from the restrooms.

I looked at D, but he didn't move, and he still seemed not to be breathing. I saw a look of pleasant surprise on his face.

"Should we...?" The question I couldn't finish hung for a moment, and he put his left hand on my right leg, just above the knee. Through my wool pants and his leather gloves, I thought I could feel a kind of shock, but one of freezing intensity.

"So surprising," he acknowledged my emotion. "Something unexpected has happened," he said. "Pull the car forward to get a clearer view; you'll want to see who emerges now."

Powered by his order, his cold reassurance, I turned the key and put the car in drive, edging forward past the pickup truck and just enough onto the grass so I could see the entire building clearly from my seat. I was waiting to collect my wife, and yet I was still frozen with fear of Justin, both for myself and for her. If I could watch just a few minutes longer, we would be together. I would shield her, take her home. She would want to see me. She would be joyous. I would rescue her. I would forgive her. I would beg her forgiveness for not having done so before. I would make promises I would keep. There would be no resignation. There would be no secrets, no barriers to our confidences. There would be joy and safety. Only joy and safety. Joy and safety.

And there was a vengeful joy in my mind: Robert was dead.

But then I looked up and saw Robert, alive, standing on the narrow, sheltered landing in front of the cinder block building's water fountain. He was holding the two backpacks.

"Catherine?" I screamed out, still seated, still wearing my seatbelt. Why didn't I get up? I looked toward D as I reached to unhook myself and run into the shelter. He seemed to shimmer and then to fade. Robert walked to the passenger side of the car and bent down to talk to me. I couldn't remember how to open the window, so he opened the door, and slid into the passenger seat as D flickered out of existence, absorbed by my growing understanding and escalating horror.

"Catherine!" I screamed again, right in his face. The syllables bounced around the car and echoed in this small section of the park off the barren brown and gray winter surfaces.

"She's not here. She's—" He put the backpacks carefully between his feet on the floor of the car. In his right hand was a gun, some kind of pistol. "Justin is dead, and this is over." His words were brazen and masterful, but he wilted into the seat, and his left hand shook as he steadied the topmost pack in front of him.

"I saw her. *I saw her go in!*" I screamed again. "I smelled her perfume. She's here." I looked behind me to my dogs watching me. They had smelled the Shalimar, hadn't they?

My jaw dropped as I wondered wildly — had he had killed her, too?

He shrugged dismissively, finding me no colleague, no confidant, and began to get out of the car almost immediately, but he stopped himself and spoke outward, as if to the pickup parked now slightly behind us.

"She's not here." His voice sounded as if it came from the depths of vast oceans of exhaustion. "I told you not to expect anything. Not to hope for her."

"I saw her," I whimpered.

"I don't know what you saw. She's dead. Justin gloated to me right before I shot him. They killed her within a few days. They didn't know what to do with her. He bragged about it. They couldn't have let her go anyway. She's dead...buried. Somewhere in Two Rivers Park." He allowed himself to collapse back into the seat for just a second or two, took a breath, and then clicked the trunk opener of his car and began to stand up.

"But...D. D said..."

"D? Who is D?" He was throwing the packs into his trunk and covering them. "This was a gang of three murderers — and whatever else they were — and now they are all dead. They killed each other. And I killed the last one for my son because couldn't get his own revenge." His voice was hardened, biting.

I scanned frantically the lot and the surrounding park, but I knew there would be no D in the car or behind Robert or in the grass going down to the shore. He'd come from somewhere like that black and white dream world from my adolescence, and, at least for now, he had faded back into it. I had no reply to Robert. I couldn't process all that was happening.

I took another tack; I didn't want to be alone. Without D, even Robert was better than silence.

"They'll find you. You just shot that guy! You did something...something with Catherine. The police will find you." I wasn't ready to let go of Catherine. I knew I had seen her. And at the same time, I also knew he was right, that I would never find her.

"Don't worry about me," he said, turning and bending down, putting his head back into the car, speaking quietly, mindful of the public nature of the park, the devastation behind him in the shelter. "I just shot the guy who killed my son. Nothing's going to happen to me. If I were you, I'd get out of here, though."

I don't remember exiting the car, taking the steps into the shelter, or pulling open the door to the bathroom. But I remember what I saw there: the sprawling diminished body of Justin, folded against the back wall, with a cement block divot where the bullet had exited his head, and a blood smear trailing the paint where he had slid down the wall. His left leg was unnaturally bent, and his arms rested at gravity-produced angles that signaled pain in the living, and protest in the dead. The vanilla-colored walls reflected the natural light that squeezed in through sliver windows toward the roof in strange strips of shadows and brightness across his torso.

My wife was not there. There was no Shalimar or daffodil scent in the room, just the putrid smell of the toilets and the dead, damaged body, the room pulsing with my heartbeat and the rhythm of my lungs.

I emerged out to the fresh January air and stood on the landing. In that moment, my emotions were indescribable. Now, when I think about it, I can put into words some of what was flying around my mind, but some of it is still just a wash of feeling. I wanted revenge on Robert so much. He would pay. I could make him pay. I knew. I knew it all, and I could actually make him pay this time. He would be brought down from his mighty perch, vilified in the local media, a villain. And his affair with Catherine would be part of the sordid tale. It would probably take a back seat to the murder, but it would be intertwined with the story, and it would be a big story, at least here in Arkansas. But at the same time, he had killed my wife's tormentor; he had acted with reasonable vengeance on the man who had unleashed all this violence on my quietly broken marriage. Robert had ended it all.

And from some latent, silent, saddened place in my brain I heard the words of Dr. Robeson telling me that forgiveness was the erasure of a debt that was owed. I could see Catherine looking at me there in the office, her eyes full, hopeful but measured. I could not see Robert now, and perhaps that was better. Looking at him was an exercise in hatred. But finally, here in this gravel parking lot, with a man dead in the building behind me, my wife dead somewhere beyond us, I understood what this would mean, that I had the power to forgive Robert, and in that moment, in that decision, after all this time, to forgive Catherine. And not just to think it, but also to act on it, to do something that would create the world I walked into and inhabited for the rest of my life.

I felt wherever my wife was, she, too, had been liberated in that instant.

Robert didn't wait. He saw my face, and got into his car, which he started without preamble, and sped out of the lot. I followed suit to Chuck's car.

I drove automatically toward Broadway in North Little Rock and took the Broadway Bridge into downtown Little Rock. I called Chuck to tell him I was all right, and we could come exchange cars later that day.

"I'm glad to hear from you..."

"We'll talk soon, Chuck. I promise."

"I wasn't asking. I... I am just really relieved."

"Everything is still really awful, Chuck, but now I know, and guess I'll be alive to live through it."

"Amen."

I hung up and remembered Robert saying where Catherine was buried, "somewhere in Two Rivers Park." I was on Cantrell, at the intersection with Tyler Street, and I could not drive one more foot westward toward that park and her lonely, empty body.

I turned right and drove north to the Catholic Diocese. When I arrived, I got out of the car and walked the lawns as far as I could until I collapsed on the winter-dead lawn behind the largest central building on campus. I lay on my back on the cold brown ground, racked with silent sobs. My gasps mingled with the cool air on the bright Little Rock winter day, as the gothic embellishments on the building pointed up into the cold January sky.

After

Mr. Catherine

9

I LOST MYSELF FOR A WHILE to the darkness. She really was gone, my efforts had been futile and she was lost to me, taken from me and lost. I'm not sure if I was really unconscious or in that liminal mental state that comes with tragedy — a timeless headspace, an eternity of emotion. I drove home on autopilot after I got up from the cold ground, turning the corners of the winding roads in the neighborhoods between the Heights and Kingwood, deadened to any thought. I drove down my street to see Brooke standing in the driveway outside her black SUV. Just standing, not looking around, not on the phone. Just standing.

I struggled out of my car, staggering toward her, the hangover that I'd been pushing back for a week with more drugs and alcohol began to settle around me. There was a vague, distant throbbing around my head and neck. My skin hurt and I felt the cold of lying on the ground seeping into my body and bones. I approached her where she stood by the open door of her Tahoe, which was still running. The heat from its interior quickly dissipated in the crystal-gray air.

"Step inside," she said, with business, but without cheer, as she gestured to the vehicle.

I climbed around to the passenger seat and found her already established in the driver's seat, turned completely toward me, her shoulder perpendicular to the steering wheel, which seemed to be squeezing her into place.

"I have less than good news, but I felt it was finally time to—"

I told her what had happened that morning, but if I thought I would see any shock or surprise in her face, I was wrong. She didn't even blink when I told her Robert Gewinn was there, so I didn't tell her why. When I told her about Catherine, she looked down at her hands, which didn't fidget with the envelope she held.

"I am sorry," she said, finally.

"I still have to tell you why I'm here. I felt it was important to tell you, and certainly given what you've told me, it may come out now, as the pieces of all of this surface, or some of them." She was so used to playing a long game, she was already processing the ramifications of this. "Of course, one never knows what will resonate with the public, or, even, what will become known. I feel I need to be up front with you so you can prepare yourself."

I stared at her, angry that she thought something, anything, she could tell me now would warrant this kind of preamble.

"I wasn't completely honest with you in terms of my current situation with your wife."

"Why? I mean, why not?" The headache pounded more loudly at the front of my head, my stomach tightened and began to hurt.

"Because I was helping Catherine, legally. She had made a decision to get a divorce. She was going to leave you as soon as she could get some things in line. She was applying for posit—"

"What? What are you talking about? No, no she wasn't. She was happy. She — that last morning, she was energetic, perky." I thought of the last minutes I had been with her, her determination and verve.

"Yes, that was probably a side effect of her decision. She knew what she was going to do."

I started to ask her another question, words were percolating up into my consciousness but I was having trouble grasping them. She kept talking.

"I have been trying to call you, not as much about this, but instead about some of the things you've been keeping from all of us who were trying to help you, and to help Catherine."

I looked down at my hands, cold and white in my lap, a chastised child.

"I can't say much more, and I'm sure you don't want to spend any more time with me than you have to, but I was instructed to give this to you today."

"Today? What about today? The significance is...?"

"Well, we were going to have things ready to initiate for the di— for the other thing today, and this was something she wanted you to have, as well. It's rather irregular, but Catherine wasn't like everyone else, of course. She really did care for you."

"Are you for real?"

She held the envelope out to me in answer.

"You're making me into a left man, instead of a widower."

"Well, legally, you are still a widower." She reached over awkwardly and patted my arm as she placed the envelope near my hands, and I reflexively took hold of it. It felt both light and heavy at the same time. "Let me know if you need something...that I can help you with." She said, and I climbed back out of the car, dismissed.

I climbed the few stairs to my front door, shakily put my keys in the door and walked into the living room, where Lavinia had to see what was going on outside. She sniffed at the envelope and wagged her tail, sniffing the air around me before losing the scent and walking out of the room toward the kitchen. I ripped open the seal and tape. There was no writing on the outside, not my name, or hers. No printed return address of the firm. Blank. The letter was undated but was definitely in her hand.

> *H —*
>
> *I felt it would be better to serve you for a number of reasons, but not because I am heartless. I know this will be a brutal shock. You are working so hard to make us happy, to put us back together, to keep us going forward. It was really affirming. And it distracted me for a long time. Your will for us to be happy was almost enough to blind me to the fact that you never forgave me, and in not doing so, you were still the master, the injured, the controller. I was worried enough that you'd leave that I forgot to ask myself if I still really wanted to stay, and when I finally did hear the question in my mind, I couldn't deny the answer. I almost couldn't hear it over the din of resignation that drowned out everything else in my life recently. But now I know. I need a new start to get back to the old me, the me you actually loved, the me you would have forgiven. The me I like to be.*
>
> *It's not your fault. I'm to blame for so much. (And this has nothing to do with Robert; that's over as it always really was). It's a cliché to say that maybe I wanted to be caught — I didn't. Hurting you like that was awful, and this is worse, so I guess I am a coward. It has to do with your power over me, as well,*

your ability to convince me of things, to talk me around to your way of thinking. But there is a fresh, spring world for me. There is an academic job somewhere that I'll be good at, that I want to move away from Little Rock for, and a life to lead that is lighter, livable, which this life is not.

I wish I could make myself happy without hurting you. I've been terrible at that for a long time, so I am giving up. I'm inspired by the people we can both be without the weight of what's come between us. I will be gone, really gone now — please don't try to see me or talk to me for a while — but life is long, my friend, life is long, and I really believe anything can happen.

With love, C

As I held the note, the reality of her giving this to me, or her telling this to me, seemed so possible. Her things were still in the house; her coffee mug from the last morning was still on the counter. And I wished she could tell me, that she were alive to leave me, because it was fair, it was real, it was her. In that last year, she had tried to mold herself to something that wasn't any of those things: She had tried to pretend along with me that we were fine when she recognized the death knell of our marriage, not in her affair, but in our response to it, in *my* response to it. My control, my denial, her resignation and my refusal to acknowledge it. Somehow, this last torturous blow felt so appropriate, I found myself believing on some level that she was alive, just gone. She could still make decisions, could keep herself emotionally alive, could make herself happy, just as she had always been able to do, when in the end, I could not.

I folded the letter and put it back inside the mangled envelope.

I remembered her recent words — old to her but new to me, though not as new as these — from the earlier journal. I rubbed my fingers together to evoke the scent of dried daffodil and thought of how she promised herself she would not raise that fear in me, that it would be too cruel, and how I ran to her and what it meant to her, what it would have meant to her if I had done that after her affair, run to her, not caring what anyone thought, run to her when she disappeared by telling the police everything, abandoning so much to love her.

She is out of my view for now, and the wait for her will be excruciating, but if I see her again, as she emerges at the top of a little gold-covered hillock, I will run to her. I will run, and I will tell her what she needed to hear from me, of my love, of my forgiveness, of my regret. I will run.

Acknowledgments

I could not have completed the first draft of this novel or the subsequent revisions without the help, support and encouragement of many people. I must first thank Dr. John Vanderslice, who so expertly designed the novel-writing class that was part of my MFA program at the University of Central Arkansas that I finally finished writing this story that had been in my head in some shape or form for 20-plus years. Without that class's requirements and supportive community and design, this book would still be somewhere in my brain and not on paper.

I also want to thank my very early reader and friend, Lynne Landis, whose enthusiasm for what I was doing with the story and love of the character D helped me commit to the strange gothic turn the manuscript took from the path I had initially steered for it. I also had other early readers, smart, book-loving women, who were very encouraging: Melissa Wilcoxson, Tiffany Hadden, Sherry Booles and Chris Meech Keene.

I'm grateful to Dr. Mary Ruth Marotte, who supported me during some tough-going with the book and to my friend and mentor Dr. Stephanie Vanderslice, who encouraged me to find a publisher for the novel and connected me with Anne Bohner, whose insightful edits and suggestions helped me produce the book it is today.

I appreciate the informational support of Lauren White Hoover and Det. Tommy Hudson, both of Little Rock, who helped with legal and police background information, as well as Malinda Moses Schmidt for neighborhood insight.

I'm so thankful for my editor, Simone Slykhous, at Creators Publishing, for her careful reading, keen eye and helpful edits.

Finally, I'm grateful to my husband, Jay Ruud, who read every draft, supportively and critically, gave me notes and tasks to complete at each stage of the game, and found a way forward for me when I was overwhelmed with revision anxiety. Without him, this lifelong goal would have stayed a dream instead of becoming a reality.

About the Author

Stacey Margaret Jones grew up in De Smet, South Dakota, or the real-life Little Town on the Prairie. Her retired-librarian mother kept her in the best books from childhood to young adulthood, cultivating a love of reading and writing that now lies up there with her love of dresses and dogs. She and her brother and neighborhood friends used to play "college" with encyclopedias, which probably was a predictor of her two undergraduate majors, elementary education and English literature, and two master's degrees, one in communications management from Syracuse University and the other in creative writing from the University of Central Arkansas.

She has worked in a battered women's shelter, a daily newspaper, a Czech economics university, state universities in South Dakota and Arkansas, a Minneapolis investment bank, an ad agency, a global marketing services company and a private school system before going off on her own to write and provide research services to marketing and public relations clients.

Jones's other avid interest besides education is travel, and she has been to 30-some countries, from New Zealand to Bosnia. She lived in Prague for a year in the 1990s, teaching English and traveling Europe with friends and family.

An introvert and the youngest in a family of nine children, Stacey has always been an energetic observer of relationships around her, and her market research career satisfies her keen interest in why people do the things they do. Her poetry, fiction and creative nonfiction focus on such observations and her interest in human behavior, particularly interpersonal relationships.

Stacey lives in Conway, Arkansas, with her author husband, Jay Ruud, and their four dogs, where she writes, runs, teaches yoga, walks dogs, obsesses over what she eats, tries to wear all her dresses, and plots her next trip abroad.

Mr. Catherine
is also available as an e-book
for Kindle, Amazon Fire, iPad, Nook and Android
e-readers. Visit creatorspublishing.com to learn
more.

o o o

CREATORS PUBLISHING

We find compelling storytellers and
help them craft their narrative,
distributing their novels and collections
worldwide.

o o o

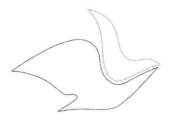

Made in the USA
Middletown, DE
04 September 2019